# DECOYS SIMPLIFIED

# DECOYS SIMPLIFIED

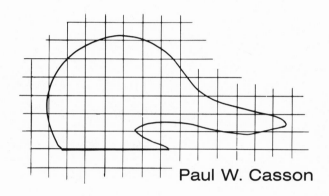

Paul W. Casson

FRESHET PRESS
ROCKVILLE CENTRE, NEW YORK

photographs and illustrations by

Dennis Buckley and the author

**Designed by John Reale**

# CONTENTS

***THANKS***
    . . . to Joe Staropoli, who started me shooting over
decoys; to Ed Urban, my almost constant duck-hunting
partner and hotshot offshore boat racer, whose seamanship
alone has been responsible for getting us back on many
occasions; to Eileen, for putting up with cork dust in
her laundry area downstairs; and to Cousin Caroline, who
expertly typed the whole manuscript

## Introduction

Why would anyone want to make his own decoys? There are several good answers to that question, besides the obvious one that duck hunters need decoys for their sport. I know of some naturalists and biologists who use decoys to bring birds down to where they can be observed and photographed. Also, decoys are currently much in favor as home decorations, and there are certainly enough species of ducks to fit in with any interior color scheme. Some people get a great deal of satisfaction from making things with their own hands, and a good number of home-shop buffs are always looking for something new to make. But regardless of any of the secondary reasons for making decoys at home, it is of course the duck hunters who have the greatest interest in decoys and use by far the largest number of them.

Now why would a hunter want to make his own decoys? A desire to save on the cost of ready-made decoys is one excellent reason, but another equally as good is that there is an added satisfaction in hunting over decoys that you've made yourself. A duck hunter who makes his own decoys often does so for much the same reasons that many fly fishermen tie their own flies. You can buy any number of species, styles, patterns, and makes of both flies and decoys, but fashioning your own brings a touch of pride that adds an extra dimension to your sport. Most store-bought decoys are knocked out in a very efficient, businesslike way, and in general their quality is good. If you want to pay for the best, you can buy some pretty damn good decoys. But—commercial decoys of a given species are usually all alike. The heads may face right, left, or straight ahead, but except for that they are usually monotonously similar. When you make decoys by hand, certain slight, unintentional variations, in construction are sure to occur, even though you might be making the same pose of both head and body for all your decoys. These differences from block to block give your rig added life.

This past winter while in New York City (for the day only, thank you), I visited one of the best and most expensive sporting-goods stores in this part of the country. After looking over a splendid collection of outdoors paintings on exhibition there, I went to the room where the decoys are kept. The display of the various popular species in cork, plastic, and wood must have amounted to several thousand decoys. Most of them were well constructed, but their conformations were thoroughly stereotyped. There was hardly a turned head in the crowd. There were no sleepers, crouched snoozers, preeners, feeders, guzzlers, or any other forms that differed a feather from the few conventional poses. As I looked about the room, I thought that if the whole mess were set out in the water to form one huge raft of the size one might see during migration, what a dull-looking raft it would be. You wouldn't have to be a very clever duck to know that something was amiss. I think that too much sameness in a raft of decoys can give an impression of tension, even though the heads are all at a so-called relaxed angle.

When I first started to make decoys, I made them of wood, since that was the usual method and there was very little information on decoy construction available at that time. I made solids and two-piece hollow and three-piece hollow models, but always of wood. When I began using cork, I found that I could knock them out much faster and so could get far more decoys completed each winter. Also, I had fewer problems getting the pieces to fit. I found too that I could carry a great many more cork ducks up and down the beach at low tide. And in spite of the examples, lore, and traditions of the old wooden decoys, it turned out that the cork versions appeared more lifelike in the water.

I am not the first decoy maker to use cork for decoys, and certainly I don't have the last word on decoy construction. As I've said, when I first got the decoy bug, there was very little information available on decoy construction, and all the instructions I could find had to do with wooden models.

After going over this material and studying all the store-bought machine-made decoys that I could get my hands on, I began to experiment with making decoys from cork. I continued to study the various types of decoys that I came across, as well as examining pictures of decoys in magazines and in books on the history and collecting of decoys. I made them in a number of different styles and kept correcting my methods until I thought I had worked out a pretty good system. Still there was no printed information available to help. Finally I happened on to a couple of decoy shows that not only interested me very much but also gave me an opportunity at last to compare what I was doing with the work of other decoy makers. Decoy shows cater mostly to wooden decoys, but they usually attract some decoy makers who prefer to use cork, and I have met enough of these cork enthusiasts to have had frequent opportunities to compare notes. (Incidentally, the wooden decoys at these shows are often remarkable examples of the craftsman's art, and the competition is keen. If you want to make decoys, it would be well worth your while to attend a decoy show. The detailed carving and painting of these wooden decoys are sometimes perfect. So perfect, in fact, that if you owned one of even the so-called working decoys, you probably wouldn't want to set it in the water.)

I discovered that what I thought was a pretty good system of decoy construction was being repeated all over the country by many other hunters, all with similar methods and aims. I was amazed at how small were the variations in procedure. The basic ideas were all much the same, but still there was no published instruction available for the beginner. It is because it took me so long to perfect a decoy for my own use that I decided to attempt a book on the subject. I hope it will be useful in helping new "duck nuts" get started on a fascinating aspect of their sport.

I have selected the patterns used in this book because they produce what are to me the most correct decoys. They are the result of boiling down dozens of other methods as well as incorporating my own thoughts on the matter. After studying the birds on the water, making field notes and sketches, and poring through all the books that I could find on decoys and decoy collecting, I reduced my findings to the patterns contained in this book. To be sure, dozens of versions were thrown away in the process. I remember in particular one winter day several years ago. The season was over, and I had gone to the beaches to look over the ducks that were wintering there. I studied them through the binoculars, made a few sketches, came home—and threw away at least a dozen heads and made new ones. Then I repainted my entire rig. I had shot over this rig for quite a few years, yet I felt I had to correct it, since its discrepancies from the real birds bothered me. I like to think I've had better shooting over these decoys since then. I have even made a few minor changes in shapes and construction techniques while putting this book together. I think I have something good now—effective decoys that are relatively easy to make.

One of the best reasons for making your own decoys is economy. You can build a sizeable, attractive rig for far less money than it would cost to buy a similar setup. Not counting your time, you should be able to make the cork decoys described in this book for about $1.50 apiece for the ducks and only a little more for the geese.

I don't intend to run through the history of the decoy in this book. That's not my purpose, and besides I'd make a pretty bad historian. There are several really beautiful books available on the history and art of the decoy, and they make absorbing reading. I strongly recommend that you browse through some of this material before starting with your own decoys. You will get a sense of the whole game of American waterfowling as you follow the evolution of the decoy. The duck decoy is a truly American invention. It goes back to the Indians.

Rigging decoys—that is, setting them out—and all the scuttlebutt that goes along with this art will also be little discussed in these pages. There are a couple of good books already available on rigging, and in any case no one would agree with my conclusions. Rigging is the most controversial and personal aspect of using decoys.

I suggest that an aspiring decoy maker read this book through before starting on any of the patterns. Information given for one particular pattern can frequently be applied to another, though it may not be repeated in detail for every pattern.

## Materials and Tools

The decoy cork used almost exclusively today is known as refrigeration cork. It is made of cork chips and grindings that are treated against decay and compressed into boards 1' wide, 3' long, and from ½" to 4" thick. The 4" thickness seems to be very difficult to obtain, but I guess that if you push and prod your distributor, you will probably get enough for your needs. These boards are often used for insulation, bulletin boards, and, recently, on interior walls. The 2" board used in two laminated layers is best for the handmade decoy. I have seen some factory mades and a few handmades that were only 3" thick, but they did not have the convincing appearance of those that are about 4" at their thickest point.

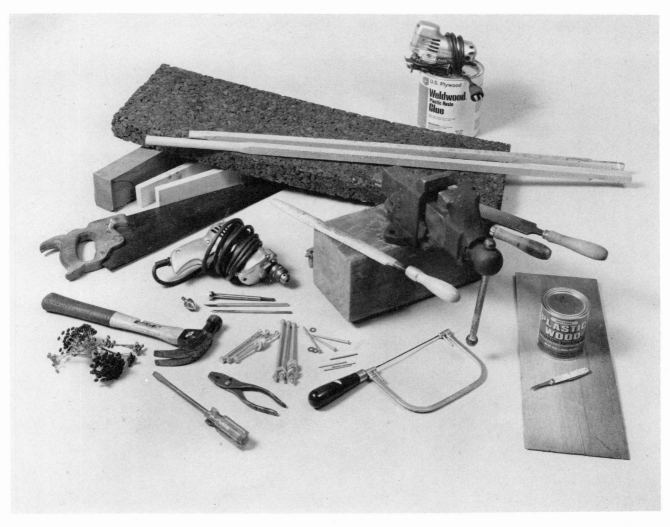

I once saw a black-duck decoy that was made of two 4"
boards and was 24" long. This was a truly outsized decoy,
and the owner claimed that he used only six of them in his
rig. But this is not the usual practice, and the plans in
this book call for the use of 2" board, since lamination adds
to the tensile strength of the decoy. Once you get the
general idea, you can take off in any old wild direction
that appeals to you.

I haven't been making decoys long enough to have
worked with natural cork in its unchipped form. At one time
that was all that was available. Today, the pieces of flotation
used around boats are usually made of Styrofoam or some
similar plastic, and it's become almost impossible to find
beat-up cork life rafts or fenders. I have been told that this
cork was the very best to work with, so if you can get some
of it, try using it for decoys. The 2" cork board can be obtained
from your local insulation firm, or you can look for it in
the classified listing in your phone book. I have recently noticed
this cork advertised for use on basement walls.

Just before this book was due to go to the printer, I was
notified by my cork supplier that a new decoy grade of cork
board has become available. It is made up of finer grindings
than the usual grade and therefore has a greater density.
It also costs more. It is called Fine Grain Decoy Cork, comes
in 4" by 12" by 36" sheets only, and costs from $4.80 to $6.00
a sheet. Our old regular refrigeration grade in 2" thicknesses
currently costs from $1.20 to $1.80 a sheet, or only $2.40
to $3.60 for the comparative cubic amount. The Decoy Grade
sands down to a smoother finish with no holes between
the chips, but is twice the cost worth the finer finish? Not
to me. And by using the larger sheets you loose the
strengthening effect of lamination.

If you have any problems locating a source of cork
board in the Northeast, try Asbestos Distributors, Inc.,
153-157 Highland Street, Portchester, New York 10573.

Wood for the heads should be white pine or cedar,
2" to 2½" thick. If you go to a lumber yard and purchase
a 4" by 4" cedar, you can have them rip it out to 2¼" or 2½",

which will give you plenty of head material. You can further rip out the thinner strip yourself to provide tail and keel material and pieces to make dowels from. Store-bought dowels can also be used; the notes on construction will show the whys and wherefores of each. A few cedar shingles (shakes) and an odd piece of pine shelving should also be obtained. When you finish reading this book and decide on your own method, you will know which materials mentioned will suit you best. A few galvanized 3" and 4" stove bolts with washers and nuts, a couple of small 1" flat-head brass wood screws, a few 3" or 3½" round-head brass wood screws together with ¾" brass washers, and a handful of 2" galvanized finishing nails should be added to your list of materials.

You should have a regular crosscut handsaw, a hammer, a screw driver, pliers, a coping saw, a half-round rasp and a rat-tailed rasp, a half-round coarse file, a small sharp knife, an electric drill, and a saber-saw or heavy jig saw or some other means of cutting through the 2" to 2½" wood for the heads. If you have access to a band saw, splendid. A good vise on your workbench is a must. A drill press in not absolutely a necessity but can be a help. I will attempt to direct you through this course of construction with a minimum use of power tools. If you have the proper power tools, so much the better; you will move along faster and easier; but if you don't have the power tools, don't drop out now. Wait until we are finished here and judge for yourself.

**Heads**

The best wood for the heads is white pine; the next best is cedar. Cedar is softer and faster to work with, and it is good enough for short-necked or crouched heads, but white pine is better for your goose heads because it is stronger, since goose decoys have such long necks. It's also good for canvasbacks, with their prominent bills.

I recommend that, before you begin work on decoy construction, you go down to your local bays, harbors, marinas, and wildlife sactuaries in the off season and study your ducks a little more carefully than you already have. Take along a pad and pencil and your binoculars. Sketch the silhouettes. Do several sketches of each species. Note head positions, tail angles, and prominent markings. Even if you can get quite close to some of those harbor-bum mallards, put your glasses on them and study their outlines and markings. It is easier to concentrate on the details through the glasses. Make plenty of notes. They will help you in making your own patterns or in improving someone else's.

When you get back from the water, remember the angles of the ducks' bills and the stretch of their necks. A calm and relaxed head should have the bill tipped below horizontal. If the bill is near horizontal, or angled above horizontal, which is much worse, you are looking at a mighty nervous duck. Its neck is probably stretched up straight too. As a rule, a relaxed duck does not show too much neck, unless feeding or preening. Those last two positions are very good additions to a rig, by the way. Decoys that imitate sleeping ducks or ducks with their heads turned back are also good. Look over a raft of diving ducks and notice the number of sleepers in the group. Sometimes they will outnumber the wide-awake birds.

As convincing as this pose may be, there will be some occasions when it will be a nuisance to use them. On a few December or January days when the temperature doesn't get much above 10 or 15 degrees—and especially while gunning for afternoon flights, when you start taking in the decoys around 4:30 to 4:45 and have a quantity to take in—sleepers and preeners tend to slow up the process, since they don't have a decent "handle" (head) to hang on to. They will also have an ice ring around their water lines, making them even harder to handle. There have been nights in January when it has taken me close to an hour to get the blocks in. What with a rough sea and the ice, I wished that I didn't have any sleepers. They are great, use them, but only in better weather. In rough weather we also cut down on the "guzzler" and feeding-goose patterns. Their outstretched necks exaggerate the front-to-rear motion, and if it is very cold and they pick up water that freezes, they look very unnatural with bills lumped up with ice.

Unless the head is stretched in one of these various unusual positions, a duck's neck usually forms a nice graceful curve rounding back in just below the base of the skull. This rounded line shows the bird to be relaxed. Note the "cheeks" —a little lower and back slightly further than you first imagined, right? Is the "nail" a darker color than the rest of the bill?

Is the bill all the same color? Or is it two or more distinct colors or blended off into darker or lighter shades at one end or the other? Do the males and females both have the same color bills? Are the nostrils near the end, in the middle, or near the head? Are any of these points really noticeable enough to even bother with? Ducks are supposed to have terrific eyesight, but I doubt whether carved-in or painted-on nostrils and nails, or even a rough indication of them, really makes much difference to a flock of divers looking you over at forty miles an hour. However, I do paint them on my own decoys because they look more correct, and the name of the game is realism. Also it helps with the painting if they are carved in or burned in. Junior's toy wood-burning kit makes the job very easy.

Having decided on your patterns and drawn them up, for both heads and bodies, trace the patterns on cardboard and cut them out. Some fellows use different types of sheet metal instead of cardboard, and some use any of the various fiber boards. My own are on ⅛" Masonite. This will give you something tougher than a piece of paper when you start mixing up your patterns and hand tools on the workbench, and will give you a firmer edge when you trace your head shape onto the wood and the pencil point bounces across the grain.

As I've already mentioned, use 2" to 2½" thick wood for heads. What we should be doing when we make a decoy, I feel, is to make a generalized cartoon of the particular species. We are striving for realism, to be sure, but only so much as is needed for the species to be recognized fast and be convincing fast, so the incoming birds can make their minds up—fast. A piece of wood under 2" will not give you a "cheeky"-looking duck. It will make a silhouette, but then you might as well use shadow decoys and forget the third dimension. You want this rig of yours to look plump, healthy, and contented, so "cartoon" the head a bit with those nice chubby cheeks. The bills that I make are slightly curved, which is not technically correct for some ducks, but when you look at a live one fast you do get that illusion. Some fellows rasp or cut out an eye slit along the head. This helps to exaggerate the cheeks and looks good. I do not cut this notch but instead make the top of the head a little narrower and let the angle from the cheek to the top give the appearance of the eye area. The main reason that I have shied away from notching in the eyes is that unless you have the notch at the exact same level and running at precisely the same angle and depth on both sides of the head, you can end up with a weird-looking head. Notching also takes time to perfect, and in this book we aim to simplify the decoy.

When you trace the head pattern onto the wood, be
sure to keep the longest lines of the bill and the grain of the wood
parallel. The bills will be stronger and will last a lot longer
that way. If you are hard up for wood and decide to use
knots, you might get away with some cedar knots, but if you
use white pine, you are sure to have trouble. In any event,
if you use a piece with even a small knot in it, keep the knot out
of the bill or it won't even make it through construction.

Trace the pattern on the block (see Figures 2 and 26;
all plans are at the back of the book) and cut the head out.
Then scribe a pencil line longwise right around the center
of the head so that the line divides the head down the middle
across the top and bottom. It would be well to remember
to put center lines down most of the pieces used in the decoy
as you get to them. The lines will continually come in handy
in centering up the pieces as they are assembled. The last
broadbill bill that I measured was ⅞ " at the widest point,
and he was a greater. Mallards and blacks are usually under 1",
or 1½ " at the most, at the widest point of their bills. Because
of this I usually use a bill width of about 1⅛ " so as to be
close to the scale of the oversize decoy and to *cartoon* them.

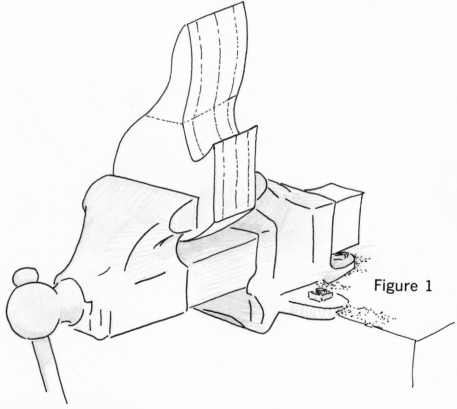

Figure 1

Measure a point ⁹/₁₆" on either side of the mid-line. At these points scribe two lines around the block parallel with the center line. This is now your 1⅛" bill width and will remain the approximate width of the forward part of the head. Mark a vertical line on either side of the face at a point where the bill would meet feathers. Carry the lines across the top and under the bottom of the block, so that these two verticals may be set at the same point on either side of the head. Now stick this head block in the vise with the back of the head only half inserted into the jaws and the bill pointing *upward*. The two vertical lines on the sides of the head are now horizontal. These lines should be well above the vise jaws and parallel with them. (See Figure 1.) Take your coping saw, with a medium-to-coarse blade (15 to 10 points to the inch), and lay it along these verticals (now horizontal) that mark the division of the bill and the head and cut straight in till you have reached the line penciled in to mark the bill width. Now, starting at the top of the block, cut straight down both bill lines till you meet the first cuts and your first pieces of scrap fall off. (Fig. 2.) The next step is to take the coping saw and, cutting at a 45-degree angle, saw off the edges around the top of the head. Go right around the entire block. Be sure to include the area under the neck edge. Taking this same angle, cut off the bottom of the neck line; it will help to give more taper for the cheek later. Looking head on, straight at the bill end of the face, you will see two shelves at either side of the bill. Cut those off at an angle, starting flush at the bill and going out on an angle emerging before the cheek. (See Figure 3 to see how the head should look at this stage.)

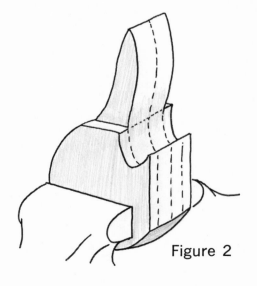

Figure 2

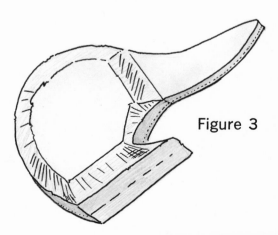

Figure 3

For the carving, some people still use a knife and some use different types of knifelike tools, some homemade. I prefer to use a half-round rasp and a vise. It may be a little slower, but it is more steady and dependable and you won't be tempted to overcarve. Your wood does not have to be the best grained either. Clear-grained, kiln-dried white pine carves well with any cutting tool, but I have some native white pine from local mills, dried in my attic, and to carve it with a knife of any sort requires a little more time, since you have to study the grain continuously. With the rasp, you "sculpt" the head. Some cedar is irregularly grained and can give you a hard time by letting itself be overcarved unless one is very careful and keeps his carving tools extremely sharp. What are known as yellow pine and sugar pine carve very nicely but are not always easy to come by in the northeastern United States.

Before you start to rasp, remember never to go beyond that middle scribed line. If you do, you will unbalance the silhouette, your pattern, the form, your duck. Don't. Another detail to remember: Quite often one side will rasp down faster or slower than the other, so do not try to compare the number of strokes in an attempt to get the same effect on the two sides.

Set the head in the vise with one jaw against the top of the head and the other jaw against the bottom of the neck (see Figure 4). Keep the mid-mark just above the jaw lines and the bill facing to the right as you face the vise and bench.

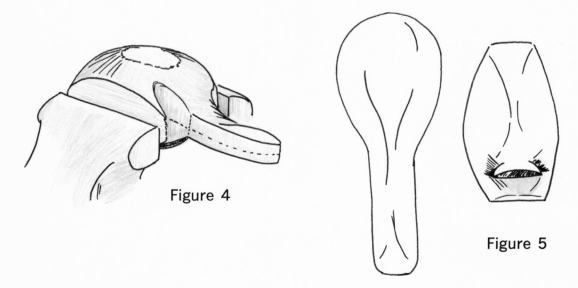

Figure 4

Figure 5

Using the round side of the rasp, work on an angle from near the mid-line of the bill to the outer bottom edge of the bill, at the pinched part of the bill. Using the flat side of the rasp, blend this gouge through the front of the face. Taper this shape from the front of the face to what will be the high point of the cheek. Shape a curve from the top side of the head to the cheek, starting at the coped line and working toward the high point of the cheek. By sliding the head more to the left in the vise, you can now round off the back of the head and neck. By positioning the head more off to the right in the vise you can get under the face and the front of the neck with the round or rat-tail rasp. Turn the head over with the bill facing left and repeat the process on that side. After this is done, set the head with the cheeks held in the jaws and finish shaping the bill with the rat-tail rasp, a coarse half-round file, or even coarse sandpaper or emery cloth. The half-round rasp is too coarse for this and might easily chew off too much wood. (Figure 5 shows the bill it should look now.)

To round off the neck up to the face and cheeks, put the head in the vise so that it is held by the top of the head and the bottom of the neck and is on its side with the mid-line at the top edge of the vise jaws. Do not chew any more off the bottom neck line; start at that line and blend up toward the cheek and face. Turn the head over and repeat on the other side.

The oval cheek areas, which should be about ½" to ¾" in diameter, are still flat. Do not worry about this, since they can be blended round after the dowel is glued and set, by holding the head in the vise by the dowel. Set the head on its back in the vise with the bill pointing upward and the bottom of the neck facing out to the right. Take your drill with a ¾" bit, mark the center of the neck, and drill straight into the head. Get the hole through the neck and into the head area, but be careful not to go through the top.

Take a ¾" stick of the original cedar or your white-pine shelving, about 7½" long, put it in the vise, and rasp it round. That is your dowel stick. Put a good waterproof glue into the head hole, push in your dowel stick all the way, and rest the head upside down to set. Some decoy men insist on putting a galvanized finishing nail through the neck to hold the dowel. The nail can be countersunk and the hole filled in with plastic wood and sanded. But a nail is not necessary if the glue you are using to hold the dowel is a good waterproof glue.

After the dowel has set, you can stick it into the vise to get at rounding out those cheeks and other fine finishing and sanding. The reason for using a softwood dowel instead of a store-bought hardwood dowel will be made clear later when we mount the head to the finished body.

You have just finished your first decoy head. There are other ways to shape a duck head, from using a sanding drum to outright carving. A sanding drum calls for another motor in the shop, and some shop skill is needed to avoid burning up the piece of wood. Carving of any sort requires a definite talent. Not every duck hunter can carve. This "sculpting" with coping saw, rasp, and vise is a nice, sure method. You can make moderate changes in the heads as you see fit. There are other techniques of rasping, but I feel that for a starter this chapter explains as simple a procedure as one could use.

### Eyes

If you have decided to use glass eyes, mark the eye spot with a pencil dot on one side of the head, place the head upright in the vise so that it is held by the dowel, and face the head with the bill pointing toward you. Hold the pencil horizontally to the point you have chosen on the one side and come in from the other side with another sharp pencil. Line the pencil points up and set the horizontal. Now look straight down onto the top of the head and, using the two pencils the same way, make your second alignment mark. Drill in the eye holes no more than ⅜", using a ⅜" bit. The glass eyes come mounted on the two ends of a soft wire. After the hole has been varnished and has dried, cut the wire to within ½" to ⅝" of the glass, put a U bend in the wire and a small bit of plastic wood into the hole, and set the eyes right into the socket. Use the point of a knife to remove the excess plastic wood as it oozes out around the eyes. Allow the plastic wood to harden, and after it has dried trim it a little more with the sharp knife point. Once you have done a few pairs of eyes you will get the hang of just how much plastic wood to use. Some fellows use painted upholstery tacks for eyes, and some omit the eyes altogether. I hunted broadbills for quite a few years with not one eye in my rig; no problems. More than half the mallards I own, both drakes and hens, have no eyes. Same with the blacks. I have never put eyes in the geese and never intend to. Every year out, at least one string of geese swims into these blocks, talking away to them as though they were long-lost buddies. This is frustrating as far as shooting goes but is very convincing and encouraging to the decoy-maker.

Eyes may be obtained through the taxidermy supply houses that advertise in the various hunting magazines. Sometimes the plain glass eyes with just the black iris are best, since a dab of the right color on the back is all that you need to finish them. This way you you can be sure of the correct color, since what you might call orange might be sold to you as yellow, etc. Herter's, in Waseca, Minnesota, handles glass eyes in what they call a decoy grade that are inexpensive.

### Bodies

Any good duck hunter can tell the difference between a puddler and a diver, even if the duck is sitting on the water at a considerable distance. The puddle ducks, or dabblers—mallards, blacks, baldpates, Canada geese, etc.—all have high-sitting tail ends and, except for the geese, their heads rest lower; diving ducks—broadbills, redheads, canvasbacks, goldeneyes, etc.—have a low tail silhouette and even when at rest their heads appear higher. In fact, broadbills, goldeneyes, and buffleheads, to name a few, actually have their tails in the water most of the time. We will go through the construction of three types of puddler bodies, in two sizes, and three diving-body types, also in two sizes, as well as the construction of the goose and the painting of all decoys.

There are other feeding positions of the puddlers—one, for instance, in which only the stern end of the duck is seen above water and another in which the entire body is visible but the whole head is submerged. We will not run through the construction of these types, since they are comparatively simple to improvise once you have mastered the basic decoy.

We will start off with the construction of the higher-tailed type, the puddlers, or dabblers. Blacks and mallards are popular examples of this type.

Making any duck body is basically a matter of gluing together two pieces of cork that are cut to the chosen pattern, gluing on the keel, and shaping and reinforcing. This is relatively simple when you are making one of those types of cork decoys in which the tail and body are both part of the same cork. All one need do then is take a brass wood screw with a washer, countersink it in the keel and through into the tail end to hold the stern section, and run the head dowel down through the keel to hold on the bow end. You will then have quite a solid decoy after the shaping. However, the cork tail ends can take a beating. If one is handling any quantity of decoys in cold weather with icy lines, in and out of boats and in and around a rocky shore, or if there is any other chance of their banging and knocking about, then a piece of wood in the tail can save you a lot of cork.

Look over your cork board carefully. One side is slightly more glossy and smoother than the other. That is the side to trace your pattern on. Lay the body pattern on the board and trace with a soft chalk or a felt-tipped marking pen. If you do not have a saber saw or something similar, the cork can be cut very easily with any kind of a saw—crosscut, keyhole, or coping saw.

### Puddle Duck Bodies

The first body we'll make is the 14" mallard-black (as we'll now call it) with an inlaid wooden tail. Copy the illustrated pattern, using a 1" grid as shown (see Figure 31). The body cork is 13" long and 7" at its widest point. Cut *two* identical pieces out of the 2" cork board and mark a center line on each one. Cut the keel (see Figure 39) out of pine shelving or cedar at least ¾" thick. Cut the keel 10½" long by 2" wide. Mark a center line down the keel piece, and using a ¾" bit, drill a hole 1¾" from what will be the bow end. Drill a ¾" hole, only ½" deep, 3¼" from the stern end.

(Both of these holes are indicates with an X in the illustration.)
Now drill a ⅜" hole through the middle of the stern hole.
Find the center point on the side of the keel (the ¾" side),
¾" from the bow end, and with a ⅜" bit drill a hole through
the two inches of wood. This hole is for the anchor line.
Run a bevel bit (the type used for countersinking flat-headed
screws) into both ends of the last hole. This will help
reduce wear on your anchor line.

Cut out a tailpiece from a thin panel of wood ¼" to
⅜" thick (see Figure 38). This tailpiece is 3¾" wide and 7"
long. Pencil a center line on the piece and put a mark
on the center one inch from the tip of the tail. To get wood
of this type, you can knock out the bottoms of drawers found in
discarded furniture, or use pieces of a gardening flat, or rip
a slab off that 4" by 4" cedar that you got for the heads.
My father-in-law gave me some beautiful big sheets of ⁵/₁₆"
wood that he had salvaged from an old piece of furniture
that his neighbor was throwing out. About three years later

I cut some tails out of it and finally got through the varnish to identify the wood. I probably own the only decoys with black-walnut tails to be seen floating in Long Island Sound.

Using the center lines to align the pieces, set the tail flat on one of the cork blocks and slide it back until the tail hangs 1" over the edge. Use the inch mark that you put on it earlier to help you find the correct positions. The tail end of the body patterns can be traced onto the tailpiece, ending one inch from the tip. This will help you to position the tailpiece more easily. Now that the tail is on the cork piece in the proper place, trace it in chalk onto the cork. Using a long sharp knife, cut along the chalked line and slice out all the cork within this chalked outline to a depth of ¾". When you cut out the two body pieces, you had some odd-shaped pieces left over. Cut ¾" strips off these, cutting parallel with the longest factory edge. This should give you various lengths of ¾" by 2" pieces of cork. Set the wooden tailpiece into the area that you have just cut out and set these last-mentioned strips of cork in on top of the tailpiece with their factory-finished side down. Once everything is fitted you are ready for gluing.

Some people use different types of contact cements or wall- and floor-tile cements. Just be sure that the one you choose is waterproof and has no asphalt in it to bleed through the paint job. I have used an adhesive called Armstrong Adhesive 520, which is used in the pipe-insulating business. I do not know if it is available everywhere, but it is great stuff if you can get hold of it. Weldwood, a plastic-resin glue is also very good. It comes as a dry powder that you mix with water as you need it. The epoxy types are also very good but are quite expensive when used in the quantities that you will need. Whatever glue you decide to use, if you have some doubts about its performance, try it out on some scrap cork first. Give it a good test to see how strong it is, how it takes paint, and whether it is waterproof.

Smear your adhesive generously on top of one slab of body cork and set the other one on it. Spread glue in the notch for the tailpiece and set the tail in. Add more glue and set the cork strips on top of the tailpiece. Put the whole package—both halves of the body, the tailpiece, and the strips—into a "press" while the glue sets. You can use furniture clamps, large C clamps with boards, or any type of homemade clamp. If you don't have clamps, you can set the whole thing on the floor and put a heavy weight on it till the glue sets. I have used all of these methods, sometimes several together.

I have a few homemade clamps fashioned in various forms by different people. You do not have to use exact dimensions, but I'll give some here just to give you a clearer idea of what the general type is like. You can carry on with whatever materials are easiest for you to come by. It's very simple. Two 1" by 3" pieces of wood 16" long are held parallel to each other by two ½" machine bolts 8" long. Set the bolt 9½" apart and use washers at both the head and nut ends. I use two of these sets to a decoy. Just slip the freshly glued block between the boards and tighten up. I recently used a 2' by 12' plank atop six decoys at a time set up on a concrete floor and weighted down with about 200 pounds of lead and iron weights.

After the glue has set in the body sections, glue on the keel, using the chalked mid-line in the cork to help center it. Be sure that the front edge of the keel on this model is set 1¼" from the front edge of the cork. Set the block upside down and put a weight on the keel while the glue is drying.

Now you will find out whether the adhesive that you used is any good. With the block still upside down, set a ¾" drill in the dowel hole in the keel (the forward hole) and go right through the two layers of cork. Then set the keel in the vise with the stern to the left and the bow to the right as you face your work. Set a handsaw at right angles to the block and cut downward across the center of the dowel hole and at a slight forward angle to a depth of about 1". Now hold the saw horizontal about 1" down from the top edge of the bow end and saw in right to left, toward the dowel hole and parallel with the cork layers, until you have met the first cut. (See Figure 6.)

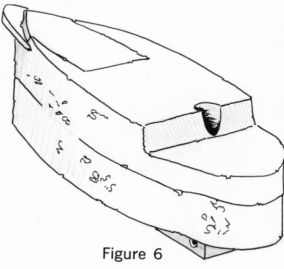

Figure 6

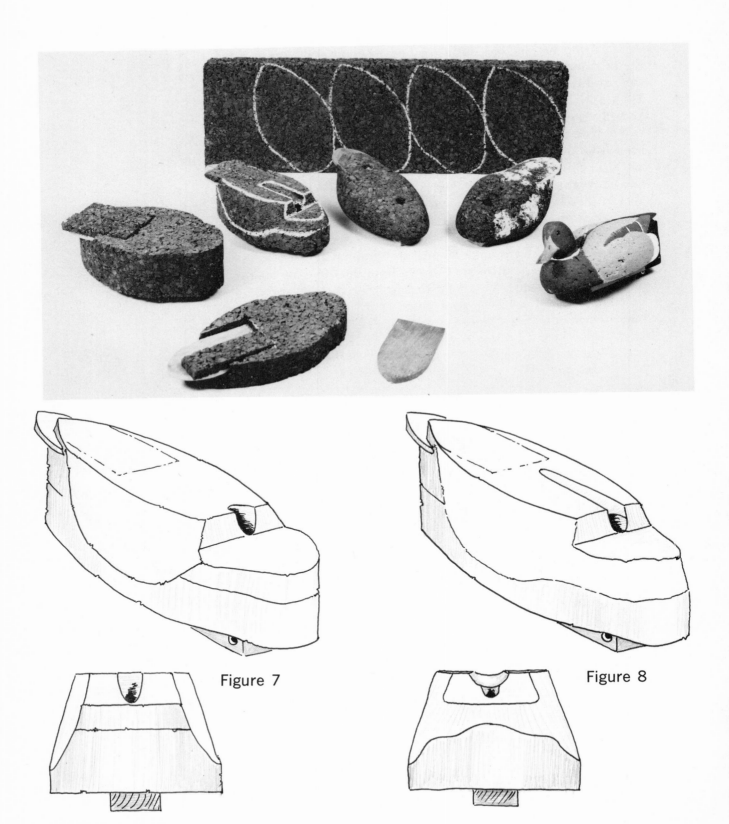

Figure 7

Figure 8

Using the flat side of the half-round rasp, start rasping the sides of the body with a top-to-bottom stroke in an area comprising about six or seven inches of the middle of the body. Stop when you have formed a plane angled from a point along the middle of the side of the bottom layer to a point about 1" in from the edge on top. Blend this plane forward as its bottom line curves slightly upward to meet the seam at the center of the bow and then work it toward the stern, letting the bottom line of the plane curve upward to a point above the place where the wooden tail emerges from the cork. (Figure 7 should help to explain.) Run the round side of the rasp across the dowel hole from front to rear at an angle that would have the rasp just about touching the forward edge of the breast and gouge a shallow trough along the top of the block, through the middle of the shoulders and halfway down the back. (See Figure 8.) With the flat side of the rasp, start rounding all sharp angles and edges. By now you should be starting to get a general feeling for the shape of the decoy, and I'll have to let your knowledge of duck anatomy take over. Studying pictures will help you with this. When you have decided that you have the top side taken care of fairly well, set the keel in the left-hand side of the vise, with the bow pointed down, and round out, or "sculpt," the rear end and slightly round off the entire bottom edge. (Figure 9 will give you an idea of how the body should look at this stage.) Do not round the side edges of the bottom too much or you will impair the seaworthiness of those flat bottoms. The old round-bodied solid-wood decoys of bygone days were sometimes referred to as "rocking horses" because of the way they behaved in a rough surf.

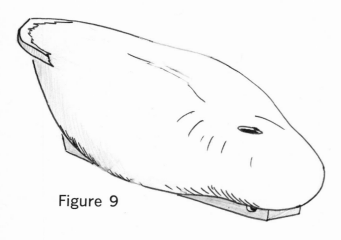

Figure 9

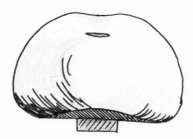

### Mounting the Head

Fix the keel into the vise with the decoy sitting there horizontal, with the bow to your right. Take a finished head, its dowel intact, and put the dowel down through the prepared hole until the back bottom edge of the neck touches the shoulders. Take a penknife or sheet-rock knife and, following the outline of the neck, cut straight downward to a depth equal with the front part of the hole. Lift the head out and put the blade flat into the hole and cut out this excess piece, keeping a level with the forward part of the hole. Blend the sharp edges of this newly cut neck area with the round side of the rasp. Set the head in place and press and twist it down until it is well seated. Keeping the head on, take the decoy out of the vise, and feed the projecting part of the dowel into the vise, from right to left so that the dowel is parallel to the floor, with the keel tight against the vise. Now tighten the vise. Be sure to have the head facing in the direction that you have chosen for this particular decoy, and bear down firmly against the top of the head before snubbing the vise up tight. Take a nail set, wood chisel, or screw driver, and with a hammer, force it between the vise

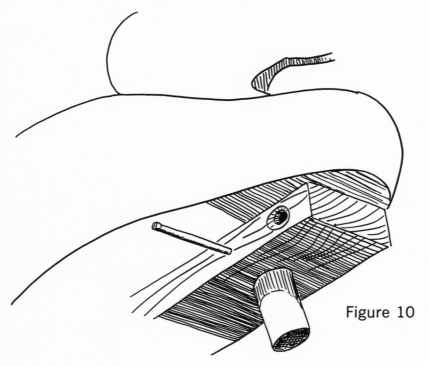

Figure 10

and keel, near the dowel. This pulls the head tightly down to the cork. While the head is held on tight like this, drive a 2" galvanized finishing nail into the side of the keel so that it goes through the center of the dowel and into the other side of the keel. (See Figure 10.) Take your new decoy out of the vise and put it back so that it is held by the stern end of the keel, with the decoy in a vertical position, the bow end sticking upright. With your coping saw or a coarse-bladed hack saw, cut the dowel off flush. If the point of the nail protrudes through the keel, file it flush to the keel. Now sandpaper the whole decoy lightly.

This is only one method of securing the head. Another is to drill a hole through the one side of the keel and dowel, using the same path as you did with the nail, and run a brass screw through while exerting pressure on the head. (See Figure 11.) In this instance a hardwood dowel may be used, since the hole has been drilled. If you use a hardwood dowel but do not drill a hole, the nail or screw will probably shatter the wood.

A hardwood dowel may also be secured in the following manner: Use a ¾" or ½" store-bought hardwood dowel and cut it so that it is about ⅛" shy of poking out from the bottom of the keel. Drill a hole, wide enough to accommodate and secure a wood screw, down into the dowel. From the bottom now send a brass or galvanized wood screw through a brass or galvanized washer that is greater in diameter than the dowel hole. Snub it up tight. (See Figure 12.) This pulls the head down snug and makes replacing the heads a little easier, when and if that becomes necessary. But the first method —using a finishing nail—probably makes the neatest package.

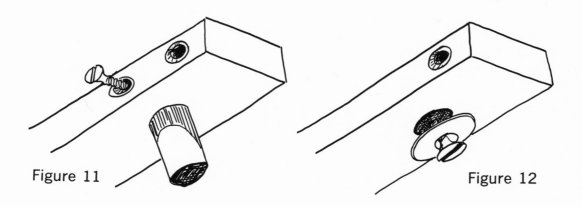

Figure 11

Figure 12

### Reinforcing

Put your new decoy in the vise so that it's held, head down, by the bow end of the keel. Send a ⅜" or ¼" drill through that hole near the stern of the keel. Drill straight through the body of the decoy and out the back. Now, using a ½" bit, drill into the first hole where it emerges in the back of the decoy and keep going until you hit the wooden tail or just into it a hair. Feed a 4" galvanized bolt through a washer and then up through the keel hole. The bolt will comes up through the tailpiece. Put a ½" washer on it, put on the nut, and tighten up. The nut and the bolt end should be concealed in the ½" hole in the decoy's back. If the countersink hole on the bottom of the keel has been made too deep and the bolt protrudes above the outline of the back, use an extra washer or so at the bolt-head end. More information on reinforcing will be given in the section on diving-duck bodies.

### Finishing

Fill in this last hole in the back of the decoy with plastic wood. Do the same with any other large holes in the cork. Also patch up any mistakes you may have made in sawing and rasping. Let the plastic wood set thoroughly and then sandpaper the patches. This material sands down much more slowly than the surrounding cork, so take care that the filled-in areas do not leave lumps on the finished surface. For all head and body sanding, I now use a sanding cloth made for belt-sanding machines. It works much better than sandpaper and will stand much more use. The type known as production grade lasts the longest.

Varnish the whole decoy and head with a good marine or spar varnish. This seals up the cork. I now use a tungseal, which is a type of waterproof varnish that is thinner than regular varnish and able to penetrate deeper into the cork.

Also, it dries faster—two coats can be put on in the time it takes for one coat of regular varnish to dry. (You can sand the roughness down and start painting as soon as the varnish has dried. We'll get into painting in a later chapter.) *Do not skip this varnishing step.* No matter how well you paint your decoy, it will absorb water if it is not varnished beforehand. Water soaked into the cork can freeze and "explode" either the cork or the painted finish. Water-soaked decoys will also ooze salt all over your paint job if they have not been varnished before being painted.

Let's go back for just a minute now. If you had a drill press, you could put a router head in the chuck and rout out the cork where the tail section goes. Just set the depth and move the block through, for a quick, fast job. As I mentioned earlier though, I prefer to describe procedures that call for a minimum of power tools, in order to show that decoy-making can be done without an elaborate shop.

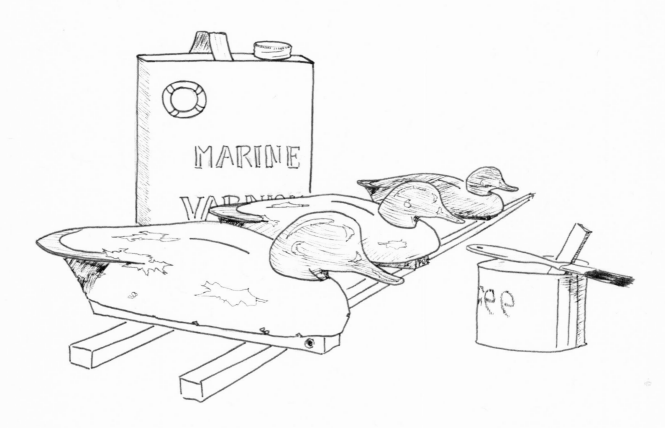

### Oversize Puddle Duck with Angled Tail

### (To Be Used Also for Brant)

The last body described had a high tail all right, but you might find that you want a sharper angle to the tail. I know a fellow who has made a jig to nest the cork block into on an angle, so that when he passes the block under his drill-press router head, he cleans out the tail section at a nice, neat angle. This does a fine job, but the router head causes extra mess, and you need extra pieces to fill in over the tailpiece. Here's a short cut which, though not as sophisticated as using a router head, will produce a body that's just as strong, if not stronger, and just as good-looking. I use it for the larger decoys, the size we like to use out on the salt water. The last-described type, those with 14" bodies, does well for us on our ponds and fresh-water swamps, but the 16" types seem to work best on big water.

Using the pattern illustrated (see Figure 32), cut out your cork body pieces. Your two cork pieces are 15½" long and 8" across at the widest point. Take the pattern (Figure 38) and cut your tailpiece from a cedar shingle with the broad end of the tailpiece at the thinnest end of the shingle. The tailpiece is 7½" long and 5¾" across at its widest point, that thin edge. Cut the keel 12¼" long and 2" wide out of ¾" stock. (See Figure 39.) Drill the ¾" head-dowel hole on the center line, 2" from the bow end and the same combination of holes for the bolt, centered 2" from the stern end. Don't forget the anchor-line hole on the side of the keel, centered ¾" from the bow end.

Take the body piece to be used on top, and chalk a line on the side of the piece, starting about 1" down from the top edge of its sternmost point and running down to a point on the bottom edge 7" forward of the stern end. Chalk the other side the same way, to guide you as you go. With a regular crosscut handsaw, slowly make your cut along the chalked line, starting at the stern and cutting forward and down at an angle, as your hand steadies the cork. It is not difficult.

Just take your time. Smear the bottom body section with glue, then take the 7" stern piece that you have just cut off and put it in place on the bottom section. Put the adhesive on top of this angled piece, set the tail wood in position on it, and put glue on the tail. Now set in the top piece of cork. Be sure that 1" of wood sticks out for the tail, as before. Set the whole package in the clamps to dry.

A little faster than the previous method? Why waste time explaining the other? Well, it wouldn't hurt to do several more methods. In doing them, as in explaining them, you come across procedures, tools, and ways of handling materials that will familiarize you with the whole game. If you try various methods, you will learn far more than the guy who is still fooling around with one type of decoy, the one he started with. He will never improve it if he is afraid to make a different move. As you become more familiar with your materials and methods, you'll be more willing to experiment and improve. For the type of decoy just discussed, the larger head, as shown in the pattern picture, will of course be necessary. The method described first is still the most satisfactory for geese, as we will see later.

The shaping procedure for 16" decoys is the same as for the first type, except that since the body is a little longer, that initial angled plane will be longer too. In fact, this shaping is pretty much the same on all types of decoys, as we shall see. We have gone through three methods of mounting heads, so choose the one you prefer. Remember that the bottoms should not be rounded too much. Keep the sides a little straighter than you might be tempted to make them, so that when you wind anchor line on the decoy, the line won't all slide down to the tail. There are no strict rules involved here. Now that you have learned the basics, you can always put the second-type tail on the first-size pattern or vise versa. Once you have absorbed the methods, alter them to suit yourself.

Glue the keel onto the bottom with its front edge set back 1" from the front edge of the cork when using puddle-duck heads (blacks or mallards), but keep the keel flush to the front edge of the cork when using brant heads.

Use a 4" galvanized bolt, and follow the directions that are given in the section on reinforcing. The only change in these instructions is in the size and depth of the top countersink hole. You do not reach the wood tailpiece on this model. A ¾" countersink hole, just deep enough to keep a ¾" washer and the nut below the surface, is enough.

### Diving Duck Bodies

The diving body shown in Figure 31 calls for two pieces of cork 12" long and 7" at the widest point. The tailpiece (see Figure 38) is 7" long and 2¾" wide. This size, which is pretty close to the actual size of a broadbill, is to be used wherever a person can manage a large raft of them. They are comparatively small and easy to handle. Use a 1½" keel 9" long with the head dowel hole centered 1¾" from the bow end and a hole drilled 1½" from the stern end to receive a 3" brass wood screw of whatever weight you were able to get hold of. (See Figure 39.) The anchor line hole is still located on the side of the keel, ¾" from the bow end.

Mark the center lines on the two body pieces, the tail, and the keel. Lay the tail on top of one of the cork pieces, in its appropriate position, with a ¾" to 1" overhang. Center it and chalk its outline onto the cork. This cork section with the tail space marked off on it is to be the lower half of the body. Cut out just enough of this marked area to set the tailpiece into it so that the tail will be flush with the top of this lower block. A sharp penknife or sheet-rock knife and the flat of a rasp should get this area of cork cleaned out easily enough. The wood for this tailpiece can be either the type we used on the first puddle duck or a cedar shake. If you choose the shake, be sure to cut the tail so that the pattern runs with the grain and the heavier end is at the tip of the tail.

Once this tailpiece is fitted flush, make your decoy "sandwich" again. Cover the bottom section with the adhesive and set the tail in. Put adhesive on the tail and set the top on. Put on the clamps. Let it set. Next, set the keel in the same

manner as before, making sure that it is positioned only 1"
from the bow edge. Perhaps you have noticed that this is
the third keel that I have designated to be placed at a particular
distance from the front edge. This is because I have asked you
to predrill the dowel, bolt, and screw holes, and if this keel
is not placed where I have indicated for these particular
patterns, the whole business will be off. I only mention this
because there is no law that says that your keel can't come
out flush with the breast. I have a few decoys on which I
brought the keel out flush, and then as the breast was
shaped I took the coping saw and continued the breast
curve right through the keel. They look nice on some types, and
might even be a little stronger, but this procedure is not
necessary. Just remember, should you decide to use this method,
to paint that keel face cut the same color as the breast itself.

The whole package has been glued and set in the presses;
the glue is now dry; you have drilled the dowel hole through
the cork, then put the block in the vise held by the keel,
stern left, bow right, as you face the decoy. Make a horizontal
saw cut into the bow, starting about ¾" down from the top
and going in parallel to the top, cutting from right to left,
from the breast to the front of the dowel hole. Then angle a
downward cut from the top back of the dowel hole to the front
of the dowel hole to meet this first cut. With your chalk, mark
a line on the side of the top section, starting from a point
about ¼" above the tailpiece on that stern edge and angling
up to a point on the top edge of the top piece about 5" to
5½" away from stern end. Mark this line on the other side
also to help guide an even cut. Use the crosscut handsaw
and make this chalked cut. Use the coping saw to cut a
45-degree angle off the silhouette under the tail. You are now
ready to start sculpting again. On this type of decoy, set the
side angle with the rasp, going from the top down. Start
amidships and chew from a point about 1" in from the top
edge to a point on the side in the middle of the lower layer.
Continue this angle from the neck hole and work around and
almost to the tailpiece. Let the bottom of the angle line that
is formed come gently up to meet the tailpiece. Sculpt the

other side to match. Put a slight horizontal crease down
the middle of the back with the round side of the rasp by holding
the rasp parallel to the block. Round the breast and blend all
sharp edges and angles, using the flat side of the rasp.
Fit the head in the same manner as before, cutting out
around the neck and "seating" it in. Sand the rest of the
block as we did the others.

On the diving-duck decoys, I usually rasp the top edge
of the wooden tail only but sand both edges. As before, use
the plastic-wood to fill all largish holes. Set the head, and before
putting the wood screw up from the keel, drill a small hole into
the tailpiece, so that the wood screw will not split it.

### Oversize Diving Duck Bodies

The next diving-duck body we will build is a little larger,
though it's handled the same as the last one until you get
to the tails of a certain species. The body pieces are 14"
to 15" long and 7¾" across at the widest point (see Figure 33).
The tailpiece (see Figure 38) is 7½" long by 4" across.
The keel piece (see Figure 39) is 11" by 2" by ¾"
with the dowel hole centered 1¾" from the bow end.
The wood-screw hole is 2" from the stern end.
On this model the keel is set back 1" from the bow edge of
the body. This size decoy is definitely oversize for most diving
ducks, but it works out well, particularly on large bodies of
water and where the competition is heavy. The difference on

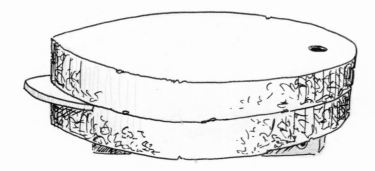

Figure 13

the tail that I indicated is this: On a few canvasbacks you should set the tailpiece flush with the bottom of the *upper* cork section before fitting the two sections together, instead of flush with the surface of the lower part. This may seem like an inconsiderable detail, but it will enable you to make a heftier-looking body, such as the canvasbacks have. For broadbill and goldeneye decoys, set the tailpiece in the upper part of the bottom cork. On this pattern I allow only a ¾" tail overhang, though a full inch would still look correct and be structurally sound. By adding about 1" to this body pattern on the stern end and using a narrower tail, say 3" to 3½" and allowing the tailpiece to overhang 1½" with a narrower taper, you could make a good merganser body that would be in scale with the others. The mergansers are sometimes used as "con men" because they are very cautious. They are also used because, with all their white, they are very flashy. This white helps to attract attention from a good distance. The mergansers are clannish, even though they will swim through any type of flock, so when setting them out, keep them closer to each other than you would the rest of the blocks in your rig. Two, three, or four are plenty.

Where were we? Oh yes, set the glued block in the vise as before, held by its keel, facing from left to right. With the handsaw make a horizontal cut from right to left, from the breast to the beginning of the dowel hole. This horizontal cut

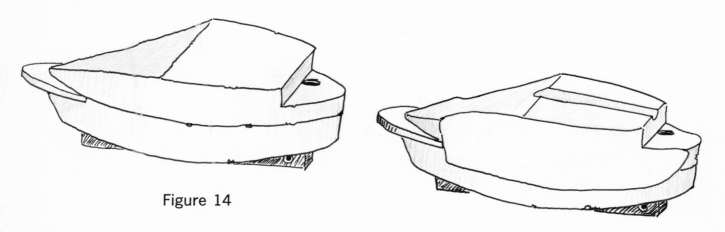

Figure 14

Figure 15

should start 1" down from the top edge of the block and run parallel to the top edge. Make the next cut downward, starting by setting the saw across the block at the back of the dowel hole and angling the cut down until it meets the end of the horizontal cut. The cut that angles up from the tail should start about ¼" above the tailpiece and go upward as it moves from stern to bow, ending at a point on the top edge from 5½" to 7" from the stern. For goldeneyes, stop the angle at the 7" mark; for canvasbacks, closer to the 5½" mark; and for broadbills, anywhere in between. The rasping and sculpting procedures are the some as for the last body type. (Figures 13, 14, 15, and 16 show the various stages.) In mounting the head, use whichever of the three methods described that suits you best.

Insert the 3" wood screw angled upward and forward from the hole provided in the keel and through the tail section, just as we did on the last type of diver. When I started making diving-duck decoys, I used to insert a bolt here, as I still do on puddlers and as others still do on divers—just as described in the first bodies in the book. Since the wooden tail is in the middle of this type of construction, and the adhesive I use works so well, it turned out that the brass wood screw, countersunk in the keel and going up through the tail on a forward angle, was quite sufficient. You might use a wood screw as large as a 3½", but 4" has been found to be too long. It protrudes from the slope of the diver's back.

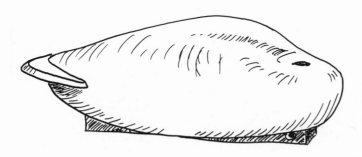

Figure 16

### Puddle Duck Body without Wooden Tail

The next body type hardly needs any explanation now that we've gone through these others. This is the solid-cork-no-wooden-tail type. The picture shows a 14" black duck (Figure 34) as an example. They both have a breast silhouette that comes perpendicularly into the water and is flush with the bow end of the keel. The similarity between them ends about there.

Let's start with the black duck. Cut the two pieces of body cork from the pattern and mark their centers. Cut a 14" keel piece 2¼" wide and center and drill the bolt holes (countersinking as on the first decoy) 4½" from the stern end and the head-dowel hole 2¾" from the bow end. (See Figure 40.) Drill the anchor-line hole in the usual place. Now center the keel and glue it on the bottom piece of cork, making sure that the bow edge of the keel is flush with the bow end of the cork. Glue on the top layer and put the whole thing in the clamps. Once it is dry, put the block in the vise, held by the keel and facing left to right. Come in with that first horizontal saw cut and the second downward cut in just the same way as on the first decoy that we did. Mark off a point on the side of the keel, 1" in from the stern end. Make a downward saw cut from the top-left (stern) corner of the block, angling down to and through the keel at this marked point. Round all sharp edges, do your modeling with the rasp, seat the head

in our usual manner, insert the 4" galvanized bolt, and
another decoy is practically finished. In putting the bolt through
this type, be sure that the buried part on the top side is wide
enough to accommodate a washer of at least ¾", since you will
not have any wood to hold against. The rest of the procedure
is the same as before. You should now be getting used to it.

### Diving Duck Body without Wooden Tail

To make the broadbill, cut out the two body pieces and
keel according to the illustrations (Figure 34 and Figure 40) and
mark their centers. Lay the body pattern on the keel and trace
the rounded shape of the tail end onto the keel. With the coping
saw, cut the tail end of the keel to this marked shape. Drill your
head-dowel hole centered 2½" from the front of the keel,
the anchor-line hole centered about ¾" from the front edge.
Glue, press, and set. Drill your dowel hole through and set
the block in the vise by its keel as before, facing left to right.

Make your first horizontal saw cut to the dowel hole, starting ¾" below the top surface of the bow, as on our first small diver. Make the second cut down from the back of the dowel hole to meet the end of the first cut, just as you did before. The next cut should be angled up from a point ½" up from the bottom edge of the stern end of the upper piece to a point on the top 6" in from the rear edge. Shape as we have been doing, starting by rounding and blending all sharp edges and angles. Round the tail area down as in the picture. Seat and attach the head. At a point in the middle of the back and about 3½" in from the rear edge, drill a ¾" hole about ½" into the cork and at a slight angle forward. Put a ¾" brass washer on a 3" brass wood screw and push the screw down through the center of this hole, maintaining the forward angle, until it hits the keel. Then screw it into the keel.

This last method of using the wood screw can also be applied to the two previous divers. A hole large enough to allow for the screw would first have to be drilled in the wooden tail, so as not to split it. Fill this hole in the back with plastic wood. (This is another example of mixing up techniques to work out one's own method. I have tried where possible to mention several ways of doing each process. Once you know a few of the various ways of constructing a decoy, you can devise an entire system to suit yourself.)

Some fellows secure this diver's tail by simply driving a galvanized nail straight up from the keel through the tailpiece. I do not recommend this method. Still others drill a hole through the keel at this stern end, drive a stiff wire up through the cork, make a loop in it after it comes through the back, and then force it back again so that the looped part digs into the top like a large fence staple. About an inch or so of wire is left hanging out of the keel. This is bent over and hammered flush into the keel. I think this procedure is "for the birds," but not for our decoys.

Now let's get back to that last decoy without the wooden tail, which we haven't finished yet. Reinforce the tail end by making a "plaster" by mixing your cork grindings and the adhesive and smearing it into all the holes in the stern. After this dries, sand and varnish the decoy as before.

## Coots

Coots in a decoy book? Who'd shoot one? Who'd try to eat one? I know that I wouldn't waste my time on them, other than to casually observe and study them. But there are hunters who use coot decoys almost exclusively, and both puddlers and divers are decoyed in to see what the coots are feeding on. Other hunters use a few coots scattered through their rig to indicate the presence of a good food supply.

I have never used coot decoys, so I can't properly dispute their value. I designed the head pattern given here (see Figure 28) and adapted it to the smaller diving-duck body (with or without the wooden tail) at the request of a friend who wanted a few. This fellow swears by them. Maybe they're helpful, maybe not. It is because rigging is such a controversial matter that I stated earlier that I did not intend to discuss it extensively. I suggest that you stick with whatever system of rigging that works best for you. If you are just getting started and have not established a proved system of your own, consult one of the several good books on rigging that are available.

Whatever your opinion of him, the coot is included here for the sake of completeness and to help the hunters who view him favorably.

I have given only one coot head pattern. It may be used facing either forward or slightly to the left or right. I don't think it's necessary to have a preener or a sleeper for this bird. Let the duck decoys take care of casual appearances. If this fellow is supposed to be such a voracious feeder and if his presence is supposed to suggest an abundance of food, then the regular head is all that should be necessary, since he should have either just surfaced or be just getting ready to dive.

Use either of the smaller diver-body patterns for the body. Set the tails and keels in the same way as before. The only differences are in the initial handsaw cuts.

Set the glued block in the vice by its keel with the bow end on your right and mark chalk lines across the top surface at points 3½" in from the stern end and 3½" in from the bow end.

The mark near the stern end is to indicate the point where the tail-angle cut ends on the no-wooden-tail model. This cut should start on the stern end ½" up from the bottom surface of the upper piece of cork. The mark near the bow end is where a cut goes straight down to meet the breast-shelf cut that comes in from the bow end. This breast-self cut is made parallel to the top of the cork at a depth of ¾".

The rasping procedure is the same as that used on the diving ducks. If a point about 6" in from the bow is kept as the highest part of the back and everything is rounded down in all directions from there, you will come close to the round-blob shape of a coot.

Painting this one is very simple. I didn't even use eyes on the ones I made. Paint the whole thing black, then paint the bill white, extending the white up toward the crown of the head. After the black has dried, lightly drag a brush with a little dark gray on it over the black body. Don't put any gray on the head.

The live bird has a white underside rump patch and a brownish eye, and sometimes the top edge of the bill is brownish too, but for a hunting decoy the painting pattern given is sufficient.

### Three Ply Goose

Are goose decoys practical? Are there enough areas where geese can be decoyed into floating blocks? Whether or not you are hunting in an area that is heavily frequented by geese really does not matter. They are still the biggest con men in the business. At the end of certain hunting seasons, when the only season open was for broadbills, I have used a half-dozen goose decoys in the shallow water to make the ducks more confident of the rig, only to find blacks and mallards landing right in with them.

There has been quite a bit of talk recently about the use of jumbo, or "magnum-sized," black and mallard decoys of from 20" to 24". The claims made for these are that they can be seen from further off and that you need fewer of them. This is very probably true. After all, we have just gone through the making of 16" decoys, which we know are oversize, and we also know that this has been going on for some time because they work. But the jumbo idea is not new to hunters who have been using a few geese in their rigs. Depending on what you are hunting and how you rig up, if you use from

three to six geese in your set-up, with those big white rumps, light
fronts, and white cheek patches, not to mention their size,
you cannot help but attract the attention of incoming birds.
Besides winning the attention of the new arrivals, goose
decoys, will give them plenty of confidence, since the goose
is known to be wary.

The procedure for constructing the heads is pretty much
the same as for ducks, except that there is more neck. I settle for
a full 2" board for these heads (see Figure 27), and so far have
used only native white pine. Be sure that the grain for the
"guzzler" position goes the length of the neck, head, and bill.
If you should find it difficult to get one piece of wood to
accommodate the upright position, don't be afraid to use two
pieces. Just be sure that the grain runs with the length of the
lower part. After cutting the two pieces for this head, drill the
dowel hole right through the lower part and up into the upper
part and glue in the dowel as you glue the two sections together.
The dowel will help to strengthen the head before you start
to shape it. The "guzzler" neck should be positioned over
the hole on the finished decoy to determine where the dowel hole
should be drilled. This hole is then drilled into the neck piece
just shy of coming through. The illustrations should clarify

the construction steps, which you will find similar to those
for duck heads.

Cut out three body sections as shown in Figures 35, 36
and 37. Cut out the tail pattern as shown (see Figure 27), from a
piece as close to ⁵⁄₁₆" in thickness as possible. Mark all center lines
and other measurement markings shown in the pattern.
The tail section should be 10" by 5½" by ⁵⁄₁₆". Mark a line
the length of it through its center. Put a mark ¾" to 1" in from
its stern end. With that portion of about 1" hanging over the
stern end of the top cork section, center the tailpiece on top
of this cork section and trace it onto the cork with chalk.
This traced area of cork is now removed to a depth of at most
¾". Use the same procedure as described earlier for the 14"
puddler. Glue the mid-section to the bottom section after
lining up their bow ends flush with each other and lining
up their centers. Glue the top section to the mid-section after
making their stern ends flush and lining up their centers.
Glue in the tailpiece. On top of the tailpiece, glue in strips
of cork of about ¾" that have been cut from scrap
(see Figure 17). Don't worry if these pieces of cork stick up
higher than the rest of the block, since you can shape it
back down later to blend in with the back contour.

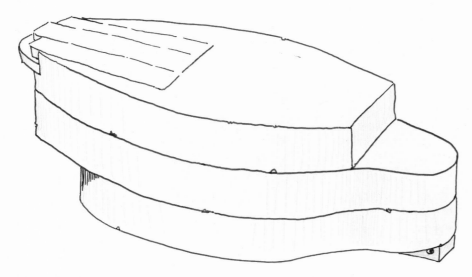

Figure 17

The keel (see Figure 40) should be 2¾" by 15" by ¾" with the countersunk bolt hole drilled in the center, 2¼" from the stern end, and the ¾" head-dowel hole centered 4¼" from the bow end for the regular head, or 2¼" from the bow end for both the feeding and sleeping poses. Don't forget the ⅜" anchor-line hole centered on the side of the keel at least ½" back from the bow end.

Glue on the keel after setting its bow end flush with the bow end of the cork and centering it up with the body. Clamp the whole jumbo sandwich until it sets.

Drill the head-dowel hole through the two cork layers, using the dowel hole in the keel for a guide. Carefully, make a handsaw cut on an angle on the top section as shown in the picture (see Figure 18). Start on the top at a point about 5" back from the front of the top section and cut down on an angle to the front of the top section's bottom edge. This is done while the rough block is held in the vise by its keel, facing left to right, as we have been doing with every other body block so far. Change this position now and put the block in the vise, still held by the keel but with the bow down and the stern up, on the right side of the vise as you face your work. Make a coping-saw cut starting where the cork ends on the underside of the wooden tailpiece and cutting through the top and mid-sections on a line that meets the top stern edge of the bottom section. Continue this cut through the bottom section to the stern end of the keel and take about ⅛" off the top stern end of the keel. (See Figure 18 again for an example of how the block should look now.) Using these cuts on this set of patterns, you can see your goose begin to emerge before you have done any real shaping.

When you round the front of the block, round the keel to the form. Rasp down the form using the same general method as with the puddler ducks. As mentioned before, the patterns and the cuts are the important part of this type. By just rounding all the angles and edges on this form you will almost be there. Use the pictures (see Figures 19 and 20) for a guide, and move slowly. It will really surprise you to see how fast this goose block will finish up.

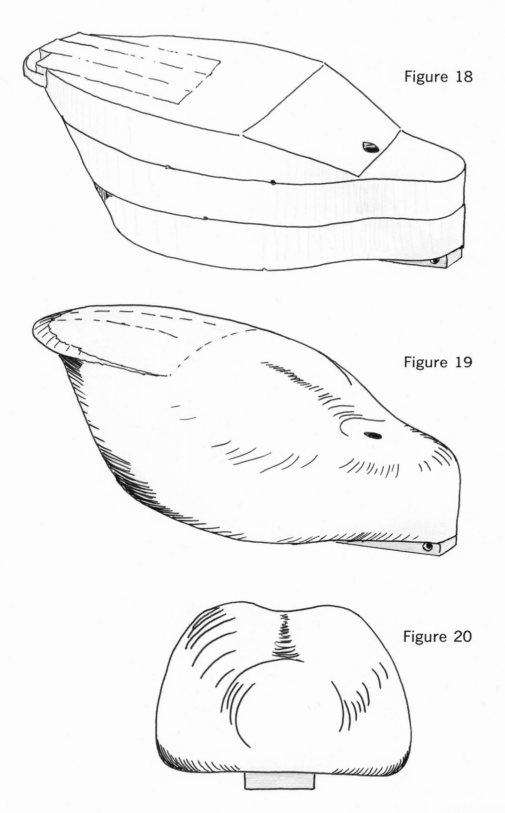

Figure 18

Figure 19

Figure 20

You will have to set the head in a few times and shape the breast to it. Remember to keep the sides a little straighter than you might be tempted to do, in order to be able to wrap the anchor line around it later without having it slip. Be especially careful not to overround the bottom edge of this decoy, since an object of this size with a rounded bottom will really rock if the water gets rough. Rasp a slight trough behind the neck on the slope of the back. Leave the keel flush in front to help reinforce the comparatively narrow and longish breast end. Lock the head in with a galvanized nail, as was demonstrated in the chapter on Mounting the Head. Use a galvanized 6" bolt through the stern end of the decoy, as in the puddle ducks, and be sure to put a washer on both ends of it. Fit it first, and if an extra washer or so won't keep it below your finished back surface while still countersunk in the keel, you may have to hacksaw a little bit off the top end of this bolt. After the bolting and head section are finished, fill in any bad holes and cracks, in and around the tail section in particular, with plastic wood. Sand the decoy after the plastic wood dries, and then apply the varnish. A light sanding after the varnish has dried will remove the "burr." It's a good idea to sand off this varnish burr. Your paint job will be smoother if you do.

This completes a conventional goose decoy. The keel with the hole through the bow end is also conventional. Whether you can use it in a conventional manner will depend on your circumstances.

I've said that I wouldn't attempt to get too involved with rigging, since all we wanted to do was to make a few decoys, but I would feel rather guilty if I didn't talk about rigging for a moment on this goose. After all, I did burden you with this 20" to 21" monster; now how do you plan to set it out and take it in?

I started out in the usual manner with the anchor cord wrapped around the body and the ring anchor around its neck. Setting them out was never much of a problem, but taking them in was another story. They are large and a bit cumbersome, to be sure. When winding them up, I would have to grab the neck in one hand with that arm extended and give myself a bath as I tried to swing the line onto it or it onto the line.

This was all done at arm's length, to avoid knocking myself in the jaw. When it was really cold and the decoys had ice rings around their water lines, the line would slip up to the neck, or too far astern, or off the decoy entirely just as I was getting the wrap started. Any way you look at it, they were clumsy to take in and very time consuming.

We have now licked the problem, and I feel obliged to pass the solution on. I don't want to get involved with the topic of rigging in general. This rigging business is not done the same all over, though it may be thought to be. It becomes a very personal thing. The critics are endless. As I have said several times during the construction phases—absorb all methods and then create a system that suits you best.

So much for the short course of Casson's philosophy and back to a goose decoy that is about to float away unless we get an anchor on it soon.

We got hold of some brass snaps from our awning, canvas-products, and sail-making friends, the last-named of which you can find located in most harbor areas. (This same snap, by the way, is the one we use in setting out our diving-duck rig in deep water when we hitch several together.) Tie one end of the anchor line to the snap and the other end to the oval ring anchor and wrap the line around that anchor. On the last wrap, as you run out of line, secure one of the sides by putting the snap through the ring. Hold the snap in your hand with the anchor dangling. It does not unwind, right? Just put it down now and wait a minute.

Since the long keel weight for the goose usually has to be mounted forward (keel weights will be discussed in a later chapter), we use a brass or zinc screw eye in place of a wood screw in the weight's forward hole. Snap the clip through the screw eye after it has been wound in the prescribed manner. This is how we now transport the decoy and anchor. To set the decoy out, unhitch the clip, back it off through the side of the anchor, snap it back on the screw eye, set the decoy in the water, and let go of everything. The anchor will unwind itself, and the line is secure to the decoy.

To take in the decoy, grab it, set it in the boat, and unsnap the clip. Then pull in the anchor as the clip falls into your boat, and wind in the line as we did at the beginning of these instructions. Now clip it back on the goose. This saves time, keeps you from getting soaked, eliminates slipping problems with ice, and takes a little more work out of what should be enjoyment. If you are in a real hurry because of extreme cold, or darkness closing in, just drop the anchors in a pile at your feet and grab for the next decoy, instead of hooking the anchors to the screw eye after it is wound. Hook them up on your way back in (unless you are alone, of course) or after you get to the beach or dock.

### Brant

Not many duck hunters are fortunate enough to ever see a brant, much less get a shot at one. Their numbers have been considerably reduced in recent years, and so far as I've been able to discover, they're to be found only along coastal waters during the hunting season.

Their graceful and sometimes zany flight antics can keep you on edge while sitting in your blind. First they're coming at you, then they switch to the right, then to the left, then in again, straight for you. You wait . . . you're ready . . . and they flair again to one side and up in a swallowlike maneuver. Just when you think they are really air-borne, *bam,* they'll hit the water. And they'll be just out of range all the while.

I hunted outside of one harbor area on the mainland side of Long Island Sound for about fifteen years and saw brant come near us only once during all that time. Then we moved our boat a few miles down the coast for the last half of one season, and we had brant all around us every day. So you never know when the opportunity may arise.

Formerly, if I wanted to observe a brant, I would have to go down to the Jamaica Bay Wildlife Refuge to even see what one looks like. Jamaica Bay is a great place for any duck nut, by the way. It is situated between JFK International Airport and Manhattan Island and is under the jurisdiction of the Park Department of the City of New York. One March day as the flights were getting itchy for the return, I stood in one spot and, with the Empire State Building and the whole Manhattan skyline as an incongruous backdrop, counted nineteen species of ducks and geese without the aid of binoculars. With the glasses I spotted twenty-one. And for the bird watcher that is only the beginning. To observe the likes of ibis, gallinules, skimmers, and bobwhite quail, to name only a few, with that city background can be a rather strange experience.

Having gotten this far in the book, you find that there's nothing special about making a brant decoy. The dimensions of a brant body are actually about the same as those of a good-sized black or mallard. Up close, the head of a brant looks too small for the rest of the bird, and the wings are long and lanky. Brant appear to be almost all wing.

The oversized puddle-duck body with either of the two brant head patterns (see Figure 28) will give you a decoy of the same size as a real brant. My own first brant decoys were just a couple of old large mallard blocks to which I added new heads and new paint. The only way the large puddle-duck body is altered for this purpose is that the keel is mounted forward, so that its front edge is flush with the front edge of the cork. This will put the dowel hole in the proper place for the brant heads. Since you probably will not be making too many brant anyway, it will not be necessary to bother with figuring out new keel measurements. This forward keel edge can be rounded with the rasp during construction, so that there will be no hard edges and corners protruding.

The procedure for the heads is the same as for the duck construction. The sleeper-preener heads can also be mounted facing forward to represent a feeder. Both positions are mounted in the same dowel hole that is used for the regular upright-head pose.

I started out using full 2" white pine for these heads, and it was fine while it lasted. After it ran out, I switched to cedar cut from a four by four. The sleeper-preener-feeder head pattern fits onto a 4" piece of wood, and it is comparatively easy to line it up longwise with the grain by turning it one way or the other. To make the upright headpiece, take two pieces of the ripped-out 2¼" by 4", glue the 2¼" sides together with Weldwood, and put them in clamps. This will give you a section of wood 2¼" by 8". This same new board can also be used as stock for the geese. Go through both pieces when drilling the dowel hole through the finished head. This, plus the dowel, plus the glue for the dowel, will reinforce the two-piece head. When you arrange the patterns on this newly fabricated plank, try to avoid waste by placing the pattern so that you might find room for a shorter duck head in a corner or under the curve of a goose neck.

When rasp-shaping brant and goose heads, you can use the method of marking the high cheek point and working everything down and away from it, just as is done in constructing regular duck heads. You will end up with a good working-decoy head, and your construction time will be fairly short. For added realism, you can do more sculpting beyond the jaw and skull line if you have the time and the hands. Since both geese and brant show a lot of neck, this extra modeling may suit you better. However, the simpler method will give you a very serviceable working-decoy head in the shortest, easiest manner.

I have never put in nostrils or used eyes when painting brant. Just use the basic paint pattern, set your keel weights, rig your lines, and you are all set to go.

### Painting

Varnish all surfaces at least once with a good waterproof varnish to seal up the decoy before painting. Decoys should be painted with a durable paint that has absolutely no gloss or shine to its finish. As you have no doubt observed by now while studying your bird shapes and patterns, bird feathers do not reflect light. There is never any glare evident on the feathers

of any bird. When you look at a multicolor bird, you can see
the individual colors because their finish is dull and doesn't
mirror sunlight. True, you may see iridescent sheens on certain
parts of some birds, but this is something else again, and
you can still read color. When a decoy, dull paint and all,
gets wet, it shines excessively. This shine is extremely unnatural
and causes ducks to flare.

There are several companies that supply a very good
grade of "decoy paint." One is the Parker Paint Company,
Main Street, Oshkosh, Wisconsin. Another is Herter's, Inc.,
Waseca, Minnesota. Both companies supply kits for whichever
species you are interested in. These kits include patterns for both
drakes and hens. Herter's also sells individual colors in bulk.
Both houses are very reliable, and there are no doubt a few
others around. I have used paint from both of these sources
but have also gone into mixing my own colors and arriving
at my own patterns. Start with a quart can of a good outdoor

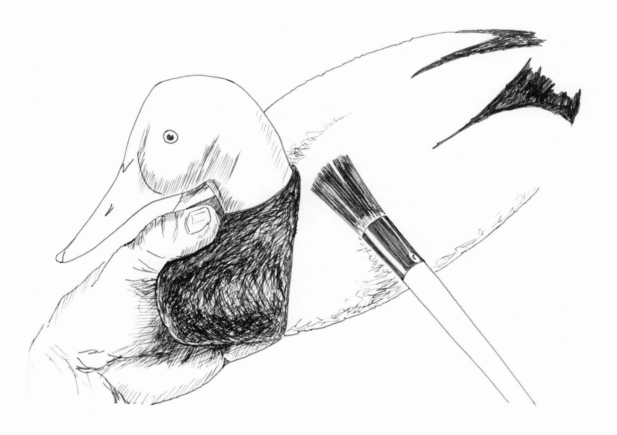

flat black and another of flat white, some tinting-oil tubes of burnt sienna, burnt umber, yellow ocher and Prussian blue, some turpentine, and some Japan drier. With this collection you can mix up any of the dull duck colors that you may need.

The color patterns illustrated do not include every type of duck ever shot at. I have included only the more-popular species. Many ducks will come down to a rig of decoys of a species different from their own. Buffleheads, for instance, will decoy to any type of diving-duck rig, though some hunters won't even shoot at them. The herring gull is included (see Figure 29 for pattern) because he makes a good con man when sitting about 100 feet ahead of the rig. It's also useful to have an extra gull or two sitting around the rocks or blind that you shoot from. The color of the mature gulls in winter is just a dirty version of their summer color, so be sure to smudge up the white somewhat. My own gull bodies are nothing more than the puddle-duck body with a long tail and a different head.

**BLACK DUCK**

**CANADA GOOSE**

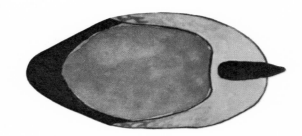

**PINTAIL DUCK**

**PINTAIL DRAKE**

**DECOYS SIMPLIFIED**

**GOLDEN-EYE DRAKE**

**GOLDEN-EYE DUCK**

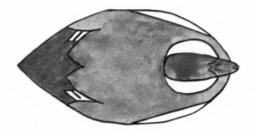

**BROADBILL DRAKE**

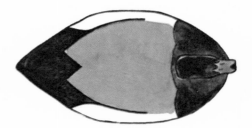

**BROADBILL DUCK**

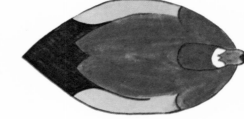

**DECOYS SIMPLIFIED**

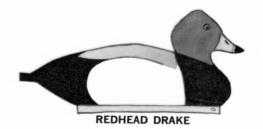
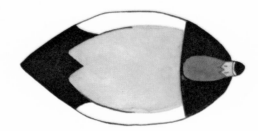

**REDHEAD DRAKE**

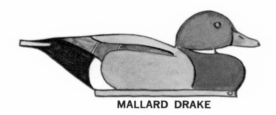
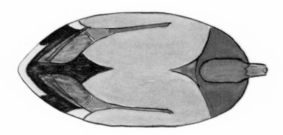

**REDHEAD DUCK**

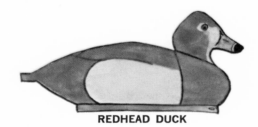
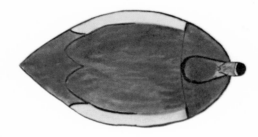

**MALLARD DRAKE**

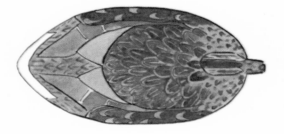

**MALLARD DUCK**

**DECOYS SIMPLIFIED**

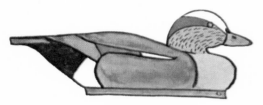

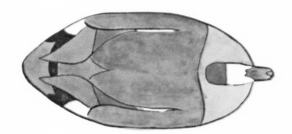

**WIDGEON DRAKE**

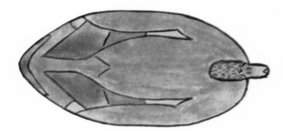

**WIDGEON DUCK**

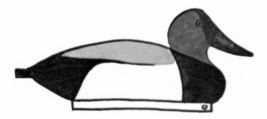

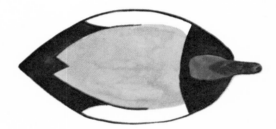

**CANVASBACK DRAKE**

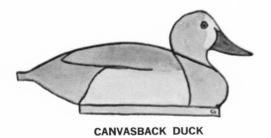

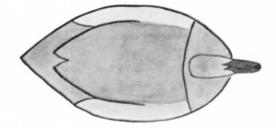

**CANVASBACK DUCK**

**DECOYS SIMPLIFIED**

The baldpate, or widgeon, is included because it too is considered a con man of a sort by some, even though there may not be enough near you to hunt. They usually rob the diving ducks of the vegetation that the divers bring up to the top, and their presence, some think, indicates that there is food on hand, thus helping to bring a flight down to the rig. This sounds plausible, but I have had no personal experience with them. Their pattern is here should you have need for it. Just apply it to a puddle-duck body.

Over the years, many tricks and special tools have been used in the painting of decoys. Not every one is capable of doing a fine job of applying these painters' techniques. Don't let that bother you. You can paint a very convincing pattern with a single brush. But for whatever interest they may have, and to give you something to play with after you have gotten caught up in decoy making, I will describe a few of these special techniques.

To put the wavy lines in the coloring on some birds, such as on the back of the broadbill, a special combing tool was used. To duplicate it, break off about 1" to 1½" of a coarse hair comb. After a black coat of paint has been put on the decoy and has thoroughly dried, apply a coat of white over it. As the white paint starts to stiffen up, scrape a wavy swath across it with the piece of comb. Wipe the comb piece clean with a rag and make another pass across, following the lines of the first. The dried first coat of black will show through the wavy openings in the white, giving you a gray cast from a distance.

Paint a piece of wood a dark brown (burnt umber), and let it dry thoroughly. Over that put a coat of light gray warmed up with a little yellow ocher. While the second coat is starting to stiffen up, take a toothpick or a wooden match shaved down to a point and pick out this second coat of paint in short, straight lines about ¼" to ⅜" long. This gives you the face of the black duck. The hen-mallard face can be done in a similar way, using more of the ocher color over the burnt umber. I have tried this quite a few times, and it turns out quite well. I have also painted these streaks on. Painting makes them a little thicker, to be sure, but is passable for the purposes of decoying.

Those breast- and side-feather arcs can be put on uniformly by using a type of twine. Using a piece of braided or three-ply cord about twice the thickness of your anchor line, make an arc the size of the feather markings that you have in mind, then pour a little ocherish paint onto a coffee-can lid. Touch the surface of the paint with your arced string held in the desired loop, and lay out the impression on the already dried dark coat of paint on the decoy. You may repeat this many times and come up with a covering of uniform "feather" marks. These twine arcs may be made up in various sizes and for safe keeping tacked at their ends onto a small piece of wood.

These methods of putting on paint designs have been handed down through generations, not necessarily by decoy makers but also by house painters, decorators, and furniture men. They will probably be found in one version or another in most books dealing with making or collecting decoys. On my own decoys I usually use flat colors and omit the combing.

The few feather arcs I use are usually painted on with a No. 7 artists' round sable brush.

On the black-duck and mallard patterns I have shown the wing speculum. The mallards have a white bar on both sides of the patch, separated from the blue by a thin black line. The black duck does not have white bars, and his blue patch is usually almost purple. Most mallard decoys have these speculum patches. But when observing any group of mallards, just try to find this patch on them as they sit relaxed on the water. You will hardly ever see it. In my own rig I have put this patch on only one out of every four mallards, male or female, and the only reason I have for doing so is to let other fellows know that I know that mallards have such a speculum. I put the patches on every mallard that I do for a decoration or for a gift, just because they are expected and make the decoy more colorful. Some fellows also put the white patch on the broadbill. I never have even considered doing it, since it is hardly ever observed on the floating bird.

On the "guzzler" goose, because its body is supposed to be stretched forward, I sometimes extend the bottom white up over the tailpiece in about a ¾" band about 3" long between the black primary wing feathers and the tail. Check with the illustration. For the sides of the goose, start at the breast with a very light, almost white, umber. Put a portion of this aside and darken with a little more burnt umber the part of the mix you are keeping before you. Using the darker mix, paint the remaining two thirds of the sides. The lighter first color can be used to paint the feather arcs on the darker part, and with the straight burnt umber, you can put a few darker feather marks on the stern end of the sides. Put a first coat of an ocher tone all over the back of the goose, making sure to load up all the cork holes with it. After that dries, put a browned gray coat over the back, making sure to glide over the holes, cracks, and crevices without filling them in. This will give you just the right amount of mottling on the back without having to paint each feather in. This method can also be tried on the hen mallard if you should find feather-painting difficult. Use brown instead of gray, of course, over the back and sides, and reverse the colors on the breast and rump.

On the diving-duck decoys, on which one may paint solid areas in different solid colors, start with the lightest color of the pattern and overpaint the area. After this dries, you can pencil the rest of the pattern outline onto the light first coat. This makes it much easier to paint a neat, balanced pattern.

It has often been said that many old-timers never painted the bottoms of their decoys with the belly colors of the bird but instead painted a back pattern on the underside, so that if the decoy should happen to flip over, it would not flare any incoming birds. Well, sometimes I paint belly colors, sometimes a back color, sometimes a gray, and sometimes just whatever is handy. I have no set rule. In any case the last time that I saw a keel-weighted decoy flip over, it wouldn't have mattered what color was on the bottom, because the wind had changed, a storm was starting, and we got picked up and out of there just in time.

On the drake mallard, there is a black V that comes forward from the tail. In a flock of live birds this varies from a short V just in between the primary wing tips to a long thin line right down the back, sometimes almost to the neck. If you vary this feature in your rig, it will help the set-up to appear more natural.

For black ducks, some people leave the dark cork unpainted after putting on a couple of coats of varnish and sanding off the shine. It looks okay, but I can't get excited over it. If you ever get the opportunity to use the natural cork, you might try a technique used by old-timers. They just put the gas torch to the cork to give the most perfect color for a black-duck decoy. The wing bars are not necessary on the black-duck paint job. Even if they showed frequently on the live birds, their color value is so close to the brown that they aren't really noticeable, even at short distances.

The illustrated paint patterns may appear somewhat opened up on the overhead view. This is to show clearly where the various lines go. When you begin copying the pattern onto your own decoys, locate the side-view lines first, then mark a middle line down the back and work from that line back to the side marks.

As far as color patterns go, there is still nothing like the real thing. Besides observing the live birds, as was suggested earlier, study those you have shot. Before cleaning the duck, set it on your workbench and take all the measurements you can, after putting the bird in a sitting pose. Make a few sketches on which to record these measurements, and locate the various colors, noting the different shades. After a few of these sessions, you will appreciate how the birds vary occasionally among the same species. When you have put a ruler on a real bird, you will realize how small most ducks are, compared with the usual decoys. If after a few of these sittings, or examinations of your notes, you make some corrections in your work, whether in patterns or construction or both, you will then know that your decoys are correct, and the confidence gained will help you to pass up a lot of the decoy scuttlebutt that's floating around.

I have seen some paint jobs on decoys that reminded me of the tackle shops that are loaded down with thousands of different fishing lures. As these lures are apparently designed to catch fishermen, so are these particular decoys painted, to catch unwary duck hunters. They might sell, but they won't decoy birds.

Constant observation will save you from this pitfall. Don't take my word. Go look.

### Keel Weights and Anchors

The main purpose of the keel on a decoy is to prevent the decoy from "sliding." When the wind switches, a decoy without a keel will swing around at anchor like a peanut shell.

This appears most unnatural to any incoming flight, should a change in wind direction occur at the time they are looking you over. True, decoys slide around anyway when the wind shifts, but the keels slow them down, so that the sliding is hardly noticeable. The keel also stabilizes the decoy and keeps it riding even, keeping side-to-side rocking held to a minimum. Some keels are deeper and narrower than those that I have chosen to use. Ideally, a keel similar to a sailboat keel would probably be best, but of course they would be impractical. I have found that the keel widths used here are sufficient to reinforce the cork body, and the depth is ample, provided the keel is weighted.

Like most other decoy makers, I weight the keels to give more stability to the decoy by holding it a little deeper in the water and to beef up the center of gravity, so the decoy will sit at a true level. Properly weighted, the decoy will not be as likely to roll over in rough water.

All sorts of weights have been used over the years. Pieces of scrap iron of every description have been forced into the bottoms of decoys or stapled or nailed on. Dozens of different types of nails, wood screws, nuts, bolts, etc., have been used. One of the neatest setups that I have seen was done like this—a couple of ¾" holes were drilled into the keel and wood screws or nails were set about half way in these holes; then molten lead was poured in and filled flush with the bottom of the keel. You had better be mighty sure of your center of gravity before attempting this method.

Regular keel weights are sold by the various sporting-goods houses. The lead weights are fine. They usually weigh from about 3½ to 6 ounces. On my smaller decoys I use about 3½ ounces; on the larger ones about 5 to 6 ounces; on the geese, about 7 to 8 ounces. There are some cast-iron types available for sale. They usually run the length of the keel and do a fine job. Because of their shape they behave like an extra keel. Cast-iron keels have one drawback, however. They rust up quite rapidly, especially in salt water. If you wrap your line around the decoy body, which is the usual practice, the rust will hasten the deterioration of the line wherever it touches it, and if you leave the line wrapped until next season, forget it. The line will have become so weak at the points where it was bent over the rusty keel weight that it will be worthless. Lead keels do not present this problem.

I was lucky in finding good keel weights in the smaller sizes. I happened to have a couple of pieces of concave cast iron that have a threaded hole in the middle of an indentation. These are used to weight down a spray hose in a container for one of those "trombone"-type garden sprayers. To make a keel weight from one of these, I bevel the end of a bolt, thread it through the hole so that the beveled tip just protrudes through into the concave opening, invert the weight, and pour in the lead. After the lead cools, drill a hole, to accommodate a wood screw, through the indentation in the lead. The indentation formed by the beveled end of the bolt allows for the flat-headed brass wood screw to fit flush.

To make the heavier keel weights, cut a piece of ¾" copper tubing in half the long way and cut and crimp both ends. One piece should be cut to 7¾", the other to 4½". Drill two holes about 4" apart in the long one and one hole in the middle of the short one. In a piece of ¾" shelving, 1½" wide, drive in three eight-penny nails, located to receive the two holes in the one mold and the one hole in the other. Hacksaw off the ends of the nails so that only about ⅜" sticks through the shelving. File the burr off the tubing and off the ends of the nails. Set the tubing halves onto these nails, open side up. Heat up your lead and pour it into your new molds. The level of liquid lead forms the flat side that fits against the keel, and the holes in the lead formed by the nails will accommodate the round-headed brass wood screws that hold the weight to the keel. Figure 21 will help to explain. You can make this type of mold in any size you want.

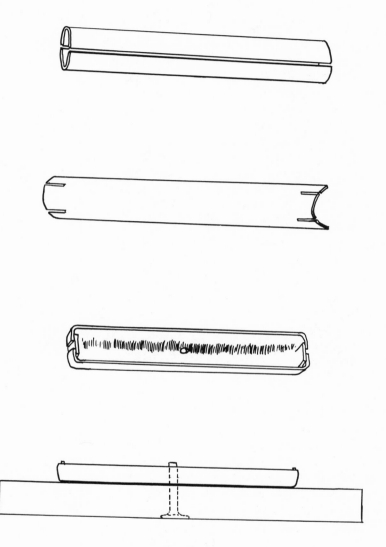

Figure 21

Once you have the keel weights, whether store-bought or homemade, affix them to the keel at what appears to be the center of gravity. Use a brass wood screw, but put it in just part way, even if that leaves the lead only hanging there. Have a basin of water ready on your workbench. It should be filled as close to the top as you can get it without spilling. Set the decoy into the basin of water. Get down to where your eye level is close to the water level. Look head on at the decoy and see whether it lists to one side or the other or sits level. If it lists to one side, take note of this but do not remove it from the water to correct it until you have checked the level the other way, front to back. You might have been lucky and put the weight in the right spot. If this is so, tighten up the wood screw, and you are finished. If the decoy does not sit level, take out the weight and adjust its position according to the list until you have arrived at a level-floating decoy. Some fellows allow for anchor pull and adjust the weight so as to have the bow end sitting a little high. I have never noticed any appreciable anchor pull unless the lines were too short, so I set my weights to give me a perfectly level decoy.

I guess everything that would sink has been used as an anchor at one time or another, but there are only two basic conventional types in use today. One is a version of the "mushroom" anchor, and the other is in the form of a ring that is put over the head of the decoy after the line is wound around the body. One mushroom type has a single stem with the mushroom end broken into six sections, or grapple-like claws. Sometimes the mushroom type is solid. Another version consists of a brass-wire ring with a simple lead mushroom attached to it. There are several versions of each type, but they are all mushroom anchors. I understand that they work very well on mud bottoms, but I have never used them, since most of my hunting has been over sand, gravel, and rock bottoms.

Before I got into making my own decoys, I hunted with a fellow who used a regular eight-ounce fishing sinker on his blocks. We never had much trouble with those. Once is a while we would have to leave one behind in a rock crevice, but not often.

I have always been partial to the ring type. One of the main reasons I favor it is that you have a neat, compact package when you wind it up. There are no dangling ends or snags. But the ring type can cause problems too. There are cast-iron rings in existence, and they are even less practical than the cast-iron keel weights that we just buried. These rusty collars will ruin your paint job after a very short time, besides rotting the line at their own knot. Another ring type has prongs on it. Though it is of lead and the prongs work well on a soft bottom, they also work on the breast of the decoy while they're jouncing to and from your hunt.

The ring that I finally arrived at is my own and serves my purpose well. I am happy with it. Help yourself. The inside oval measurements are 3½ " by 2¼ "; the sides and the string end are about ½ " thick. The outside edges of the sides meet the outside edge of the bottom nearly at right angles— slightly rounded angles, not sharp enough to do damage. This makes the bottom end heavier than it would be if round. This bottom line is also made thicker, which also adds to the weight of that end. The heavier end helps it to catch on rock or in mud or sand, should it drag in a strong sea. To make this anchor, I simply sketched it out on a 2" block of wood, gouged out the wood, and drove a nail in where I wanted the string hole to be. (Figure 22 will make all this quite clear.) After

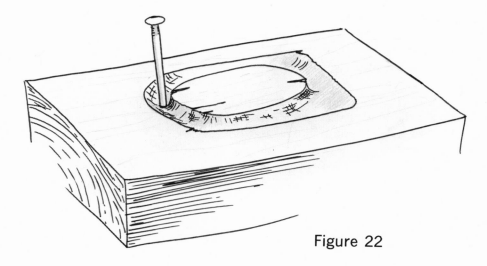

Figure 22

the lead has been poured in and has set, grab the nail with a pair of pliers and lift your anchor out of the mold. Put another nail in the same spot for the next one. I finally got around to making another mold and have poured out at least a hundred anchors in each, and though they are both charred up quite a bit they appear to be able to produce a good many more anchors. These anchors weigh about 8½ ounces. Occasionally, you might have a bit of an edge on the inside of the loop when you pour in a little too much lead. To get this soft burr off, use a short stick—one of your rough head-dowel sticks will do—and rub it over the edge. Lead is soft and will smooth down fast. If you should own an exceptionally "cheeky" decoy head, one that is too wide to fit easily through the ring, just pull on the sides of the anchor. The lead is soft enough to bend to a correct fit.

When you are hunting around for lead to melt down for these anchors and keel weights, try your local gas station if they do wheel balancing and alignment. Our local auto mechanic saves me all the old wheel weights he removes from the wheels before rebalancing them. This lead has some tin in it and by itself tends to result in an anchor that is a bit brittle in cold weather, but if mixed half-and-half with regular lead, it will strenghthen the weights and anchors enough so that they do not bend excessively. A friend of mine who hangs theater curtains and drapes saves me the lead weights from the bottoms of old curtains that have been replaced. Look over demolished buildings or dumps for the lead in cast-iron waste-pipe joints. The number of places where you can scrounge up some lead is surprising. Of course, if worse comes to worst, you can always buy it at your local plumbing supply.

To melt and pour the lead, I use a small gas bottle with a torch tip on it, the kind used in camp stoves and lamps. This is held in the vise by the tip. The lead is melted down in an old kitchen soup ladle held over the flame. This is not too sophisticated an outfit, but it has proved to be adequate for me.

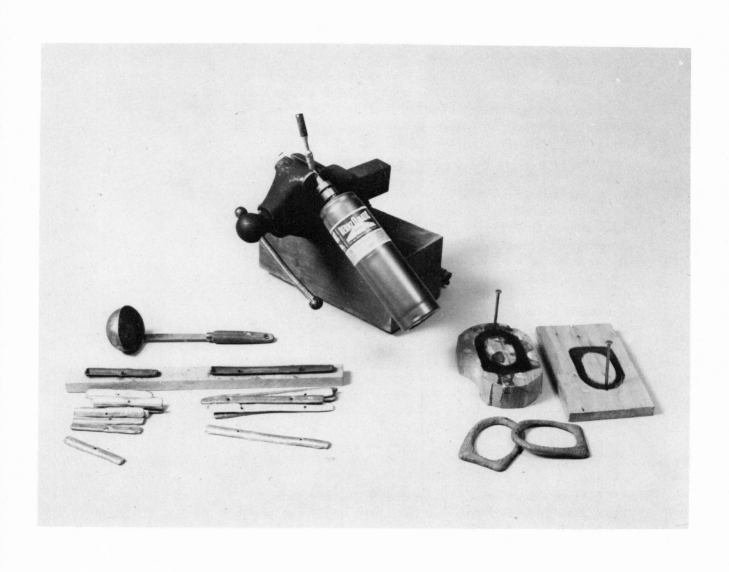

### Anchor Lines

There is not much that I can say about the anchor line, except to mention that it should be strong enough and dark in color. A rig of light-colored lines in clear water or at low tide has been known to flare ducks. I use dark-green 200-lb.-test braided-nylon line. This is not meant to imply that 100-lb. test in a dark brown is no good. A sporting goods house in Texas even sells what they call a camouflaged line, that is, one that is mottled in shades of brown and green.

I have heard that some hunters use a light chain to anchor their decoys. I just can't see why. If you were considering this, forget it. The braided-nylon line does not foul up, does not ruin your decoy, and does not add any significant weight.

In rigging up in deep water and with big rigs, brass or zinc screw eyes are sometimes put into the stern ends of the decoy keels and short lines with brass snap clips are used to hook one decoy to the other with only the lead decoy being anchored. Several of these straight lines set out can still look fairly natural if the cord lengths between decoys and the number of decoys per line are varied. There may be other ways of rigging up for this situation, but I have already gone into rigging more than I promised.

### Sleepers

When I first became interested in decoy-making, I thought that a few "sleepers" in the rig would add a different note and increase the naturalness of the group and make the whole decoy spread more convincing. I had no idea how important this pose could be to a productive set of decoys.

Through continued observation I now know that, among diving ducks in particular, many ducks in a truly relaxed raft will be seen in a sleeping pose. Notice, I said "sleeping pose."

These ducks are not necessarily asleep. They will often move around in the raft, with, against, and across the wind, maintaining this head-turned-back position. A closer look will show you that their eyes are frequently open while they're in this pose. Although they may not all be truly asleep, they are obviously relaxed and thoroughly at ease, therefore making this position an important one for a natural and convincing set of decoys. To back up my own observations, I gradually changed more of the head styles in my own rig to sleepers.

During the latter part of this past hunting season, when only broadbills, geese, and brant were open, we continued using canvasback and goldeneye decoys in the rig because of the great distance-attraction of all the white on the drakes. One morning well after sunup fourteen canvasbacks landed into the blocks, and within a matter of seconds after settling down, after some minor preening and stretching, the whole gang had their heads turned back in the sleeping pose. At the same time we had three goldeneye swimmers in the group and a pair of buffleheads cavorting around. Needless to say, the next flight of broadbills that came by didn't waste any time coming into this natural-looking rig.

After this experience, I added another dozen sleepers to my diver rig—six casvasbacks and six broadbills. At present we use at least two sleepers for every three regular heads.

When I added six more goose decoys to the collection this past winter, I made three of them sleepers.

With the puddle ducks, geese included, you will never see the whole group asleep. There is always one, at least, who is awake, preening, feeding, or acting as an outright sentry. That they are usually on shore or in shallow water, and are therefore more vulnerable to predators, may be part of the reason for this. The divers, sitting out in deeper water and secure in their ability to dive, may feel safer when resting in this manner.

This sleeping pose is prevalent among broadbills, canvasbacks, and redheads, but not among goldeneyes. The goldeneye appears content to just sink his bill into his breast while facing more or less straight ahead. There seems to be two resting places for the bill with the turned head. One is just off the center of the middle of the back, which places the bill through the back feathers and in the general area of the scapulars. The other spot is over the folded wing but covered by the overlapping side feathers. The depth to which the bill is buried into the feathers varies with the temperature. My theory is that they may be trying to keep their nostrils warm or out of the wind at least.

See what can happen to a fellow when he gets this decoy bug? Now you know why I thought that a chapter for sleepers would be necessary. The first few sleepers that I made had full-length bills with a curved bottom side to fit the contour of an already shaped notch in the cork body. A great deal of fitting and spot carving with a knife as well as a rasp was necessary, and a fair amount of plastic wood was needed to fill gaps under and over the end of the bill once it was inserted into its notch in the cork. In an effort to simplify construction for the purpose of mass hand production, I worked out my present method, which has cut the fitting time down to a minimum and eliminated the need for one to be a full-fledged sculptor.

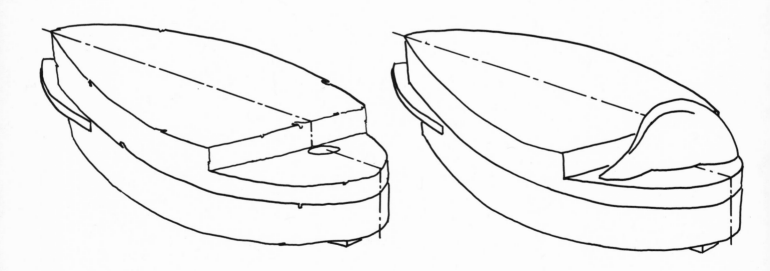

Cut out your duck-head blank from the same 2" to 2½" stock that you have been using for conventional heads. Use the patterns shown (see Figure 30), and be sure to use the mark given for the center of the dowel hole, since all the mistakes have already been taken care of for you; the various head patterns with their given dowel centers have been figured to fit the appropriate body patterns.

Make the usual coping-saw cuts for the bill and the angled quarter cuts around the top of the head and face, but do not cut along the base edges. When shaping the head, rasp to the usual high cheek area. Round the bottom of the outside cheek but not the inside cheek. The cheek that hugs the cork side is best left straight along its bottom edge. It will make a tighter fit and will not be seen in the finished product in any case.

Chalk a center line down the top of a glued decoy body that has its keel attached and is ready for shaping. Measuring from the bow, mark off the following two points on this center line. On the oversize puddler, at 2" and 7", and on the 14" puddle duck, at 1½" and 6". On the oversized diver, at 2" and 7", and on the 12" diver, at 2" and 5½".

Chalk a line that will cross the center line at each of these points at right angles. By drawing a line from the cork edge at the left end of one of these lines to the cork-edge right end of the other line, you will have the angle at which to set the head (see Figure 23).

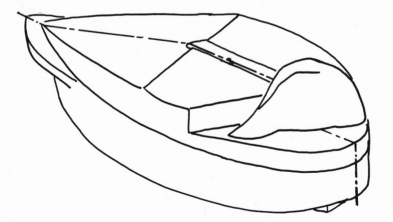

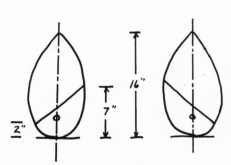

Figure 23

Set the blank decoy block into the vise so that it's held by its keel. With your cross-cut handsaw cut downward along the angle that you have marked. Cut about halfway through the top cork layer. Now make a horizontal cut through the front and side of the top cork layer until you meet the first cut.

Start rasping your body in the way that you have now become used to. Finish the sides, the rear, and the top first. Blend in the top along the new angle cut, setting the head in place every once in a while to check its fit and appearance.

After the head is permanently set, use the round side of the rasp to run two shallow gouges downward into the cork on both sides of the base of the back end of the head. Round off the high piece between the gouges and blend it into the head, rasping the head if necessary. Lastly, round out the breast shelf from the outside cheek downward, forming and finishing the breast. Walk around it and observe the finished product. Look it over carefully for any hard angles and straight lines. Round and blend any hard angles and lines.

You may need some plastic wood at the base of the head where it meets the cork and possibly at the bill end also, to help soften the original saw cut. Figure 24 will give you a good idea of how the decoy should look now.

The goose sleeper pattern is the same as the feeding-pattern head but with one minor alteration. Trace out the feeder-pattern head, then lay a straightedge along the base edge of the neck and carry this straightedge over to where it cuts across the bill. By cutting this much bill off, you now have the sleeper head for the goose. (See Figure 30.)

Drill the dowel hole into the headpiece at approximately the angle shown. Glue the dowel into the head section.

The duck-decoy sleepers described here are for the position that has the bill nuzzled in under the overlapping side feathers. Because of the size of the goose's head and neck, to do this with sleeper geese would make the decoys too difficult to balance in the water. Therefore we will place the bill at rest just off center into the back at a point that would put the end of the bill between the scapulars and under

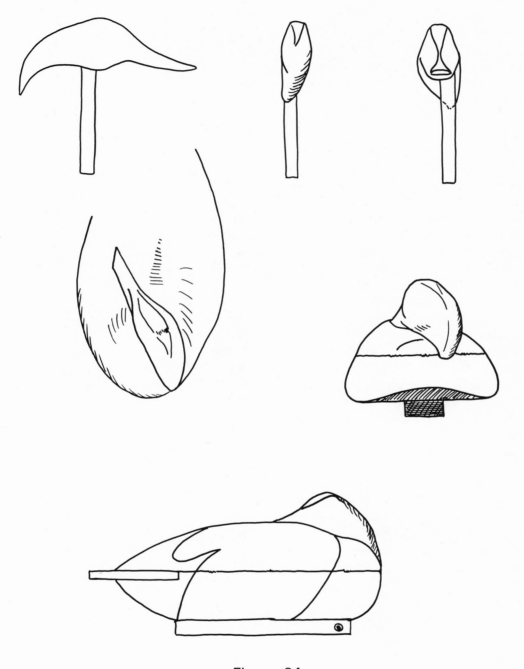

Figure 24

the secondary feathers. To get in this position, the bird usually raises the wing on that side a little higher than the other.

Shape the goose body in the way described in the goose-body chapter. Set the sleeper head into its position. You will notice that the base of the neck does not sit flush on the shelf it is to rest on.

Rasp the shelf to the proper angle to accept the headpiece. You will have to cut out a small plug on the top of the decoy to accept the short stub of the bill. Cut just enough so that the base of the neck meets the slanted cork shelf in a tight fit. When the fit looks good, lock the head dowel with a 2" galvanized finishing nail through the keel and dowel in the manner described earlier.

Blend any hard edges where the base of the neck meets the cork. You might need a little plastic wood in this area and around the end of the bill to perfect the finished bird. By rasping a slight valley from the bill back to the tail, you can create the illusion of the slightly raised wing that the head is supposed to be poked behind.

You will notice that, unlike the neck of the real bird, the finished sleeper-goose neck does not touch the body along its entire length, but it is close enough to it to look realistic and convincing from any angle. Here is one of those instances in which a compromise must be made between faithful reproduction and a practical, useful working decoy. The reason for leaving the space is to give you something to grab your decoy by. Because of their size, goose decoys would be very cumbersome without a handle.

Sandpaper, varnish, and paint the sleeper bodies just as you did with the others. Don't forget to fit these decoys with keel weights, using the method outlined previously.

I hope that once you have mastered decoy construction you will get as much pleasure from it as I have over the years. There is an added feeling of satisfaction after a successful hunt over your own decoys.

Now I'd like to make a few remarks on the hunt itself. At the rate real-estate interests are "improving waste land,"

and the way oil tankers keep breaking up and leaking all over the shore lines, we could run out of duck breeding and feeding grounds in a hurry. To help preserve the flights and to help insure your future hunting, get in touch with your local Ducks Unlimited office, and sign up. Ducks Unlimited is a nonprofit organization supported and run by waterfowlers, hunters, and naturalists alike, all over the U. S. and Canada, and it's not governmental. It's about the biggest outfit going that is really doing something constructive for the preservation of ducks and duck hunting.

### Two Foot Owl

Owls, as we know, are fiercely hated by crows, and because of this, stuffed owls and owl decoys of one sort or another have been used for years to attract crows for shooting. Why shoot a crow? One reason is that in some farm areas they not only can ruin a germinating sweet-corn crop but can also, if and when the crop matures, ruin it at harvest time. And some duck hunters justify their off-season crow shoots by remembering that crows are notorious for stealing eggs from nesting ducks. You not only keep your wing-shooting eye "in" by shooting crows but also help the ducks to raise broods for your future hunting.

Crow shooters are not the only people who have need for an owl decoy. In fact, one owl decoy could keep a group of crow shooters happy for a long time. But there are some people who have a need for quantities of owl decoys. Since the presence of any owl will scare most smaller birds, decoys of owls are used to keep pigeons, starlings, and house sparrows away from office buildings and out of airplane hangars, stables, and barns. I suppose that when so used they are not technically decoys, since they are intended not to decoy but to repel.

The body of this particular owl decoy is not quite full. It could be made fuller by using another two inches of cork, but because of its other overpowering dimensions, I did not think a full body was necessary. It is a fairly simple piece of construction if the cut-out cork sections are correctly copied from the one-inch grid and the pictures are carefully scrutinized.

The owl decoy is made from two layers of 2" cork board with a ¾" by 1' pine board sandwiched between them. You could use either a piece of shelving or plywood for the board in the middle. If you should choose the plywood, remember to use an outdoor ("exterior") type. If you were to use a piece of interior plywood, your owl could be ruined by the buckling plywood should the finished decoy ever get wet.

The wooden section is cut out to the full pictured image (see Figure 41), which is 25" long, "ears" included. The back cork section is cut out to the full image, minus the tufts, so the head is just a rounded image. This entire piece is 24" long. The front cork section is 20½", cut to the same silhouette as the back cork from the tip of its head to the line on the plan that shows where it ends.

If you should choose a 1" x 12" piece of shelving from the lumber yard, you will find that the piece is not quite 12" across. You can use plastic wood to fill in the short portion of the sides where the cork sections stick out past the edge of the wood.

After the three sections have been glued together with a good adhesive and allowed to dry under pressure, chalk a center line from the top of the head down. Locate the face radials. The bottom of the V of the brow starts at the mid-line about 4½" down from the top of the head and shoots up and away left and right at about 30-degree angles. If you have a draftsman's "30-60-90" around, it will help you get the angles right. Scribe this brow on the cork with chalk. The bottom radial line is about 7" down from the top of the head. Chalk in the rest of the radials freehand.

Hold this block on its back on your work table. Lay your crosscut handsaw along one brow line from an outside edge. Make a cut on this brow line, straight down, cutting no deeper than ¼" at the mid-point and to about ¾" at the outside end of the cut. This is the angle of the facial planes. Use the flat side of your rasp to remove the cork in shaping up this "face." Repeat on the other side of the face. Do most of your work with the body lying flat, and make most of your rasp strokes downward. In this manner you won't be as likely to lift any unnecessarily big chunks off your work.

At a point 8" to 8¼" down from the top make a handsaw cut straight across the body at right angles to the mid-line, cutting to a depth of about ¾". Make another saw cut on an angle from the bottom of the radial line to the bottom of the last saw cut.

Starting at a point about 6½" up the mid-line from the bottom edge of this front piece, use the round side of the half-round rasp to gouge a trough downward on an angle so that the middle of the bottom edge of the trough is ½" thick. Gouge this angled trough to just the width of the rasp. This is the space between the legs. Allowing for the legs to be 2¼" wide, plane an angle downward in the same direction as the trough, on the outside of each leg, using the flat side of the rasp and working at a milder angle. Have this angle start about 4" to 4½" up from the bottom edge of this piece, and leave a thickness of about ⅞" at the bottom.

Using the flat side of the rasp, round all straight edges and angles on the whole body except for the outer edges of the face and the bottom front edge of the body (feet end). Lay the decoy on its face or back at the corner of your work table so that it is easy to work around. In doing the back of the head be sure to indent slightly (about ½") at the back of the neck. Give a long taper at the bottom end of the tail.

Rasp right through the wood when rasping from back to front on that whole lower part of the tail, leaving about ½" thickness on the outer edge of the wood. When this is done, the lower portion of the decoy will have wood extending beyond the cork and will be better able to take abuse. Now use plastic wood to fill in any space between the overhanging cork layers at the shoulders.

Center a ⅜" hole at the base of each "ear," right where they meet the cork head. These holes are for the string from which the decoy can be hung. The "ears," which are not really ears—the real ears are under the radials—are angled in the manner shown so that they can act as a boat cleat would, to wind the hanging string on.

Looking at the front side of the tail now, drill two ⅜" holes, 4" apart (both 2" off center) about 2½" up from the bottommost point. These are nail holes, should you want to spike the decoy to a post, fence, or stump.

For the bill, get a pearl-like button about 1⅜" in diameter and two black ones of the same size. Take a sharp penknife and cut out a verticle notch in the face to receive these three buttons edge first. Glue the three buttons together with the pearly button in the middle. Drop some glue into the notch and push the button sandwich about halfway into the hole. Use a stick or a screwdriver to push the outer two black buttons in about ⅛" further than the middle whitish one.

Use the same-sized buttons (1⅜" diameter), either pearl-like or yellow, for the eyes. You could use taxidermist's glass eyes or just paint in the eyes, but these shiny buttons look so good that once you see them you will be sold. Grind about ³/₁₆" off one point of the edge of each large button. Get two smaller black buttons, about ¾" in diameter. Through the centers of all four buttons drill a hole wide enough to accommodate a 2½" round-headed black wood screw. Put one of the wood screws through a black button, then through the larger pearly one, then do the same with the other set.

Screw them in about 4" apart (2" each off center) on a horizontal with the bottom of the V of the brow. The ground off edges of the two large buttons should rest against the brow edges. This, at not too great a distance, gives the illusion of an eyelid.

Rasp the edges of the "ears" a bit, to eliminate sharp lines. I leave them unsanded, since the rasped edges give a fuzzy, softer appearance.

Except for the two wood screws through the eyes, we haven't put any reinforcement into this body. This is because I have great faith in the adhesive that I use. If you use an epoxy-type glue or a contact-type cement, you'll find that you won't really need any more strengthening. This type of decoy does not normally take the punishment that your duck decoys do. If you would like to beef it up, there is no reason why you couldn't countersink bolts or wood screws or both all over the place. Just remember to use large washers, to prevent the bolt and screw heads and nut end from pulling through the cork. Fill in the countersunk holes with plastic wood.

Before starting painting, you might want to seal up the cork with a coat of spar varnish, as you did on the duck decoys. This would certainly make a better job. Just sand down the varnish "burr" before painting. You will find that the easiest way to paint the owl is by hanging it by the "ear" holes and holding on to the tail with one hand. If it is laid down, you will have problems.

Start your painting by mixing up a flat-white outdoor paint with a little raw-umber tube color. This will give you a light gray. Paint the whole decoy with this, making sure that all cracks and crevices are completely filled. Allow this to dry.

Now take the same white and add a little burnt umber and a good quantity of yellow-ocher tube color to arrive at a brownish yellow for the breast and throat. Follow the photograph to paint this area. While the breast is still wet, dip the brush into straight white and blend a little into the "bib" area and into the front parts of the legs. This tends to "pull out" these areas.

Paint the face radials with a mixture of the flat white and equal parts of a little burnt umber and yellow ocher. From now on, when applying second coats of paint do not fill in the holes and cracks; just pass over them. The gray in the holes will show through and soften the texture of the finished decoy.

The brow piece should remain the original gray. Outline it with thin black lines and then outline the facial discs. By mixing a little flat white with a larger quantity of burnt umber and a squirt or so of burnt sienna, you can arrive at a shade of slightly reddish light brown with which to paint the remaining areas. Let the gray holes and cracks shine through. After painting this last color, drain and rub the balance of the paint off your brush—don't get into the turps yet— then briskly stroke the brush over the gray brows and throat area to tone them down a bit.

Take a No. 7 round artist's brush, and with the same mix that you used for the bulk of the body color paint in the breast markings and lightly paint in the radial rings on the face. Clean this same brush now and use it to apply the flat-black outlines and markings. This outlining is to add to the third dimension. Black gives an illusion of depth; conversely, the lighter the color value the more forward toward the viewer the surface appears to come. Therefore by putting the black outlines where indicated, you will make the lighter colors appear even lighter by comparison and cause them to "jump out."

I doubt whether the talons painted on make much of a difference, but to be technically correct, an owl usually grabs with two toes forward and two behind, so paint in only two. Your cartoon is finished.

Take a good, stout line 2' to 2½' long, tie the ends in the "ear" holes, and hang the decoy up. Paint this piece of line with dead-black paint. To hang the owl in a tree, use an additional length of dark line and bend a running bowline to the decoy line. I use my dark-green braided-nylon duck-decoy anchor line.

## Crows

A few crows hanging around your new owl decoy will encourage the high-flying "scouts" to come down to where they can get a better look at your owl. After the gang arrives, the crow decoys help to guide the birds into shooting range and also to keep them longer in the area after the shooting starts.

These crow decoys described here are not full bodied. Since silhouettes, as most crow shooters know, seem to work quite well, all we have done here is to give you a fuller silhouette, an almost-full body. These are a definite improvement over the usual fiber-board "flattie" and have more than proved themselves in the field.

Not counting the bills, the two patterns given (see Figure 42) are 16" and 17" long. Besides the 2" cork board, you will need a couple of wire coat hangers, a 1" by ¾" stick of wood, a few 2½" finishing nails, and a $^9/_{64}$" bit in your drill.

After cutting the bodies out from the pattern, put a short 4" by 4" or 2" by 4" in your vise, with the 4" side up. This makes a handy working "table" for the rasping, since you can work all around it. Lay the cut-out cork pieces flat on the "four-by," holding it down with one hand while rasping in a downward stroke with the flat side of your half-round rasp. Since you will find it almost impossible to do any two-handed rasping on these figures, you might try a shorter rasp than the one we have been using till now. You should be able to get five crows from one 1' by 3' cork board.

Rasp all the edges round, except for the under side of the tail edge and the bill side of the face. Leave them as they were cut. Using a downward stroke, round one entire body side and then the other. Keep the edge that you are rasping close to the edge of the wooden "table," and do not allow too much cork to hang over the edge of the wood while you are working on it or you might break a sizeable chunk off. Be careful doing the tail. Even if you don't quite round the very end of it on the top side, it will still look correct.

It does not seem to interfere with the decoy's effectiveness
if a few bits fall off the extreme tip of the tail. The paint
appears to reinforce this area enough for general handling.

With the round side of the rasp, gouge a shallow
trough across the neck on an angle using the shoulder for a guide,
as shown in the illustration. Round off the sharp edges on both
sides of this trough with the flat side of the rasp and blend
it to the shoulders and head.

Trace out several bill patterns on the 1" side of that 1"
by ¾" stick. Take your wire coat hangers, snip off the hooks
with their twisted parts, and straighten the hangers out
completely in the vise. Cut them both into equal halves. They
should be in the neighborhood of 16" or 17" each. Using
either a grindstone or a file, put a needlelike point on one
end only of each of these wires and on the points of the
2½" finishing nails.

Cut out a bill piece and clamp it in the vise so that
the top side of the bill is parallel with the jaws and sticking
out of them about ⅜". Rasp or plane the length of both
corner edges, removing wood at nearly a 45-degree angle and
leaving close to ¼" of the top plane untouched. As is, you
now have a very serviceable working bill. If you care to refine
it further by more rounding and sanding, that is up to you.

Feed the bill point first about halfway into the right-
hand side of the vise jaws, with the bottom side of the bill
parallel with the floor. Center a point ⅜" from the bottom
edge on the side that attaches to the head. Drill into this
point with your $^9/_{64}$ bit to a depth of about 1¼" and in a
direction parallel with the bottom edge of the bill. Be careful
not to come out on top.

Put a bit of your adhesive into the hole and on that
whole face side. Insert the needled-down finishing nail head
first into the hole. Now locate the nail point at the appropriate
spot on the cork face and push the nail in right up to the
wood. A small amount of rasping or sanding of the cork
where the wood meets the head will finish the job.

The coat-hanger wires are to be driven through the bodies for hanging them in trees. If standing crows are needed to set on a ground rig, just reverse the procedure and drive the sharpened wires into the under part of the decoys.

To avoid a hari-kari scene, feed the wire through with the aid of your vise. Clamp the wire horizontally with only about 2½" of the pointed end sticking out. Feed the cork to the wire slowly, holding it with both hands. As the decoy reaches the vise, remove the unit and reset the wire, again with only 2" to 2½" sticking out, and repeat until the wire is through the body. It is much easier and safer this way. For the more upright crow pose, start the wire centered in the back toward the rear of the head and emerge in the flat area át the bottom of the breast line. It does not have to emerge at a precise point to do an efficient job. On the "scolding" pose (the one with the neck outstretched), start the wire centered at a point 6" to 7" back from the bill end of the cork. Go through on an angle and emerge at the same point as on the other pose. Leave enough wire showing at the point of entry to be able to pull it back again. Use about 2½" of the pointed end to make an angular hook. This can be done by clamping the head end of the wire in the vise, which will support the decoy out from the vise at whatever angle suits you. Use two pairs of pliers, one in each hand, to create your hook. If all this is awkward for you, file or grind a point on both ends of the wire, make the hook first and reverse feed the wire through the body. If you do it this way, though, remember to cut or file off the point at the head end after you are finished.

Shape the hook so that the bottom side of the squarish U is parallel with the body surface above it and the straight point section is parallel with the shank. Push this hook up tight into the cork.

Now take the part of the wire that emerges from the decoy's back and bend the wire back slightly and bend a V into it near its middle. Adjust your bend with the pliers, so the decoy will hang in the desired position. With the scolding pose, you can leave the top piece of wire at nearly its original angle while putting the hanging V into it. Hang the decoy up and adjust it till you are satisfied.

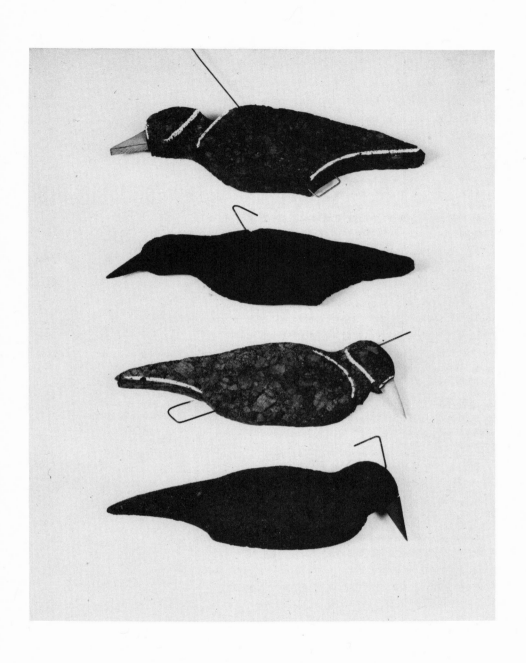

DECOYS SIMPLIFIED    91

Sandpaper, varnish, and paint the whole decoy, wire and all, with a flat-black outdoor paint.

We use ten of these crows in our rig. I guess we settled on that number because you can get five decoys from one cork board, and I used two boards when I made my originals. Ten is plenty. You could probably get away with three to six. Just remember when setting up the rig to put one of the upright poses as high as you can get it. This is the "sentinel." He is supposed to be on guard duty. His location means that it is all right for the crows to drop down to where the action is, as he is keeping an eye on things. To hang them, we use an old bamboo pole with a spike pushed perpendicularly through a drilled hole on the narrow end. A crook in the end of this spike helps.

To carry this gang, we use a "carrying stick." This is made of a 1½" wide piece of ¾" wood (more shelving) 22" long. Drill a series of ⅜" holes 2" apart and centered down the 1½" side. Find the exact middle of this stick and drill a similar ⅜" hole through the 1½" side. This center hole is put there so you can hang the whole thing up with an S hook from an overhead beam in a shed, garage, or some other out-of-the-way place. Round and sand the edges of the stick to suit. Stick the hanging wires on the decoys through all but the center hole, and there you are. Now all you need is a good crow caller to get you started. Happy hunting.

### One Foot Owl

Since you now have your crow-shooting rig completed, it ocurred to me that I'd put in this smaller owl for those of you who might want just a small fellow to keep the house sparrows and starlings out of the garage or the birds out of the vegetable garden or off the newly sowed lawn.

You will need the 2" cork board again, cut to the full size of the pattern (see Figure 43), exclusive of the "ears." This is the back section. Cut out a piece of ⅛" Masonite to the full pattern, ears included. This goes in the middle for reinforcement. Cut the front section of cork about 2⅜" shorter on the bottom. Check the pattern for locating the ¼" holes for hanging or posting the finished decoy. "Ear" holes are drilled through at about the cork line of the head, and the tail holes are each located 1" off center and 1" below the bottom of the front cork line. Again, as with so much of this decoy construction, suit yourself as to how you want to set up this owl.

After the three sections have been glued together with your favorite waterproof adhesive, chalk a mid-line the length of the front. Mark off the brow line with the V starting 1½" down from the top of the head. This brow line, as on the two-foot owl, is at an angle approximately 30 degrees from the horizontal. Chalk the horizontal line for the bottom of the facial discs about 2¾" down from the top. Mark off the top of the "bib" with a line running across the body about 4" down from the top of the head and parallel with the first horizontal line.

Lay the block on your bench, face up, and make a vertical cut with your handsaw about 1¼" deep on the "bib" line. Hold the saw on the line at the bottom of the face discs and cut downward on an angle to meet the bottom of the first cut. Set the saw on one brow line and cut so that the back end of the saw cuts in about 1" while the cut at the mid-line is only about ⅛" deep. Repeat on the other side. With the flat side of the rasp, shape down the entire facial plane on the angle of the brow cut. Lay the block on its face and with the round side of your half-round rasp, gouge out the neck line. Check with the photo on page 95.

If you round out all the sharp edges now, you will be almost finished. Keep a nearly "hard" line around the face to show off the discs better. We are not putting any legs on this little model, as they do not necessarily show on a relaxed owl. For an owl of this size the inclusion of the legs might prove rather intricate and take away from the over-all impact of the finished owl. Do most of your rasp sculpting with the model flat on the edge of your bench, and use a downward stroke as much as possible.

For "double duty," this type of owl has occasionally been made with two face sides. If this fits in with your plans, use two back sections and the Masonite, and put face sides on both pieces of cork. The only difference would be to make a 1"-deep cut at the horizontal bottom breast line and remove this lower portion to an even depth of 1".

As on the larger owl, start your painting after sanding and varnishing and patching with plastic wood to suit. Start with a light gray, making sure to fill in all the holes and cracks.

This model can be painted in gray or "red," since it is very close to being the size of a screech owl, and they have both of these color phases. The "red" is an orangy brown and can best be arrived at with your burnt-sienna tube color stretched out with a little flat white for the base, with a little burnt umber added to darken it if necessary. There is a line of light shoulder-bar markings that may help to dress it up. Outlines and other bar markings are in black. Check again with the pictures.

The eyes are made by drilling a hole through two ¾" yellow buttons and attaching them with glue and two 2" to 2½" black round-headed wood screws. The bill consists of a ¾" black button glued and pushed edge first halfway into a knife slit.

# DECOY PLANS

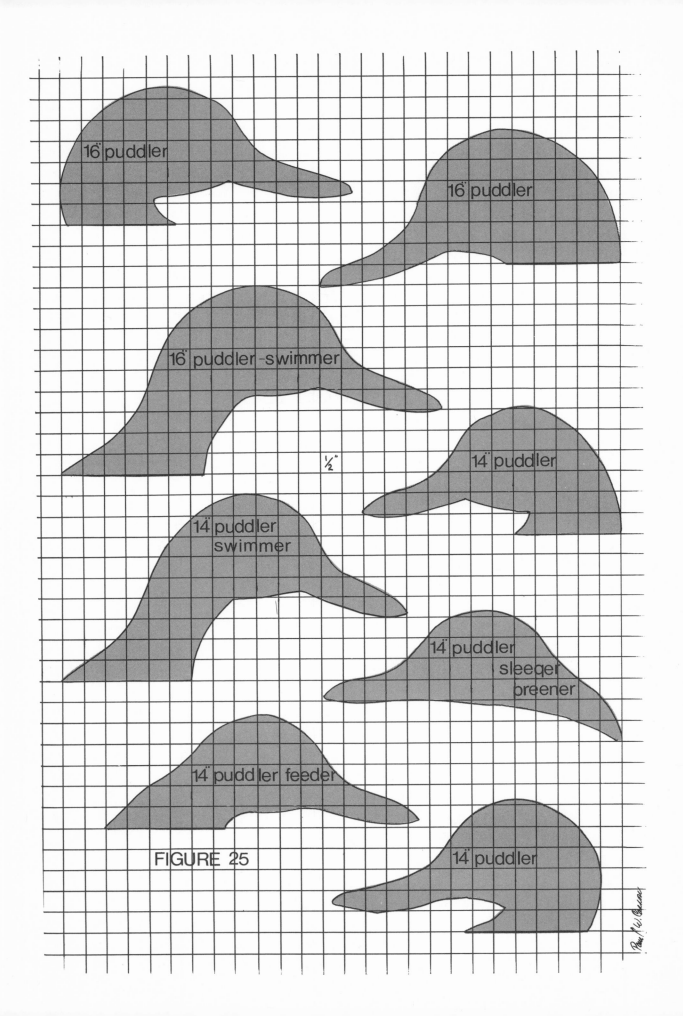

16" puddler

16" puddler

16" puddler-swimmer

14" puddler

14" puddler swimmer

½"

14" puddler sleeper preener

14" puddler feeder

14" puddler

FIGURE 25

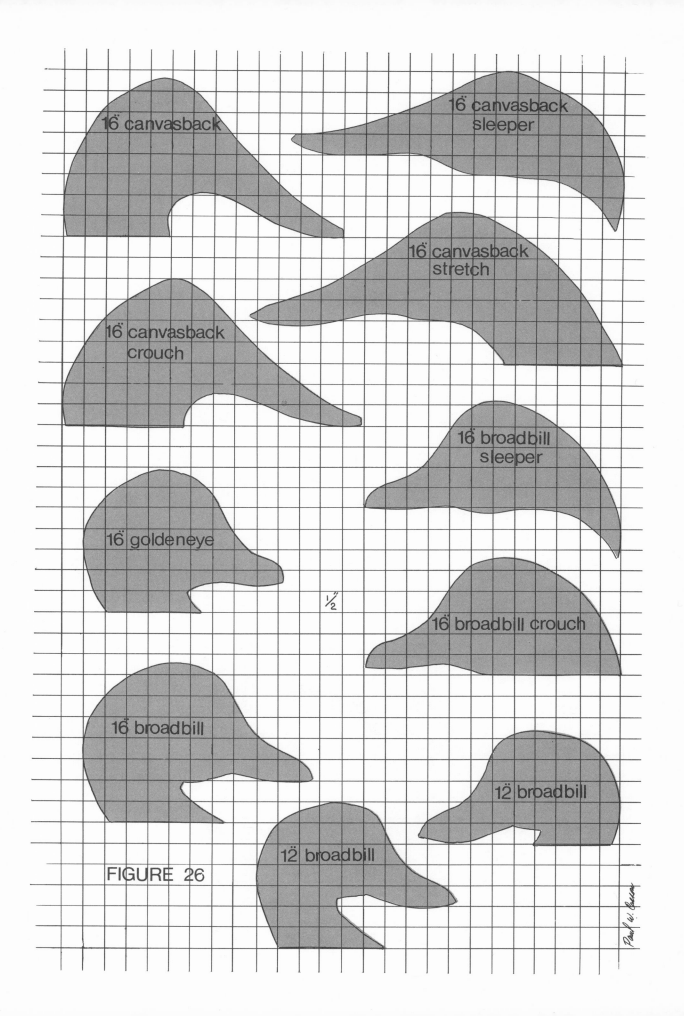

16" canvasback

16" canvasback
sleeper

16" canvasback
stretch

16" canvasback
crouch

16" broadbill
sleeper

16" goldeneye

1/2"

16" broadbill crouch

16" broadbill

12" broadbill

12" broadbill

FIGURE 26

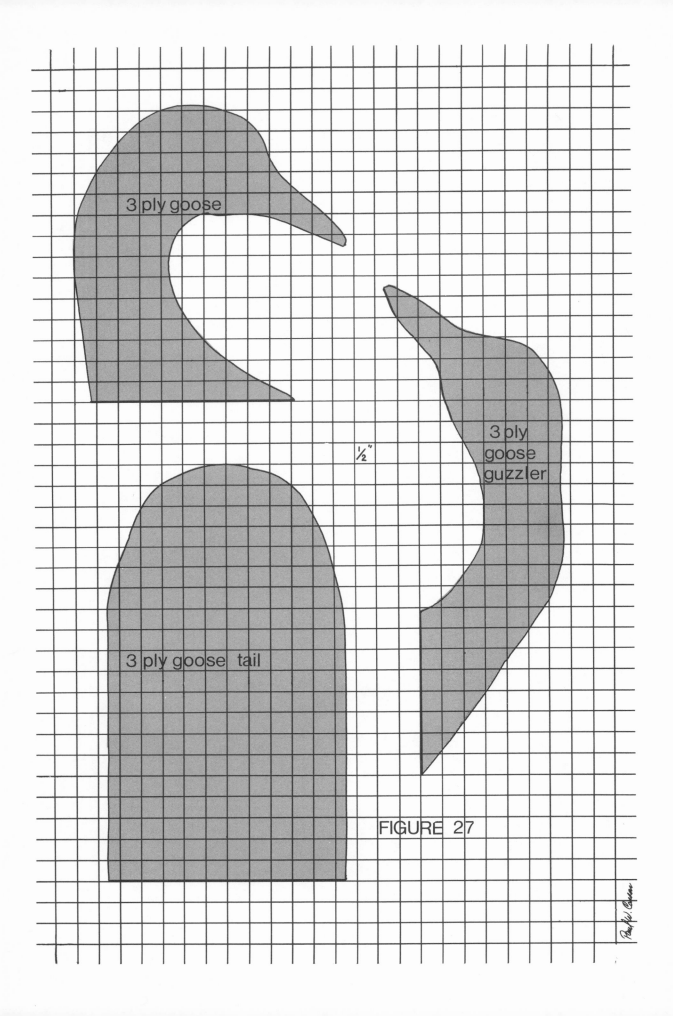

3 ply goose

½"

3 ply goose guzzler

3 ply goose tail

FIGURE 27

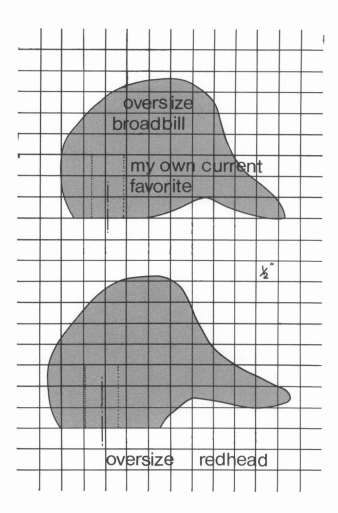

oversize
broadbill

my own current
favorite

½"

oversize redhead

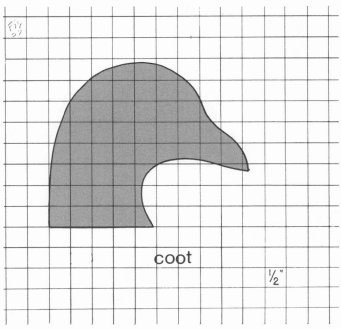

coot

½"

FIGURE 28

brant

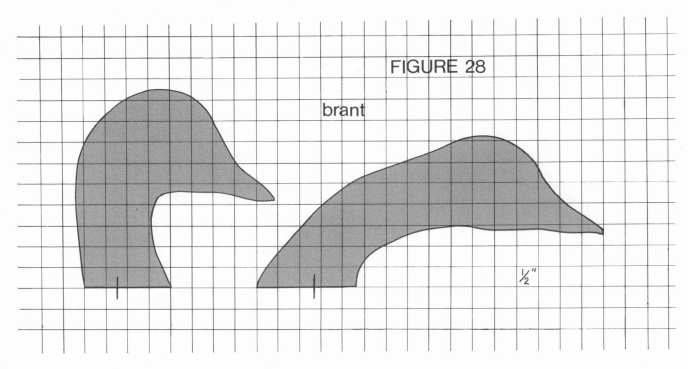

½"

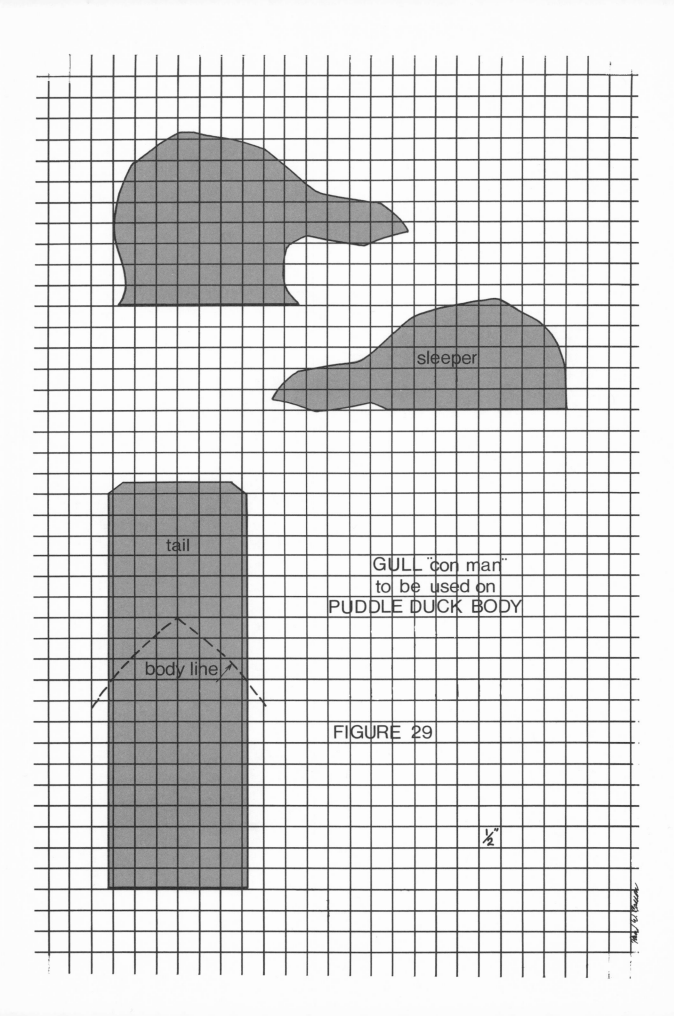

sleeper

tail

body line

GULL "con man"
to be used on
PUDDLE DUCK BODY

FIGURE 29

½"

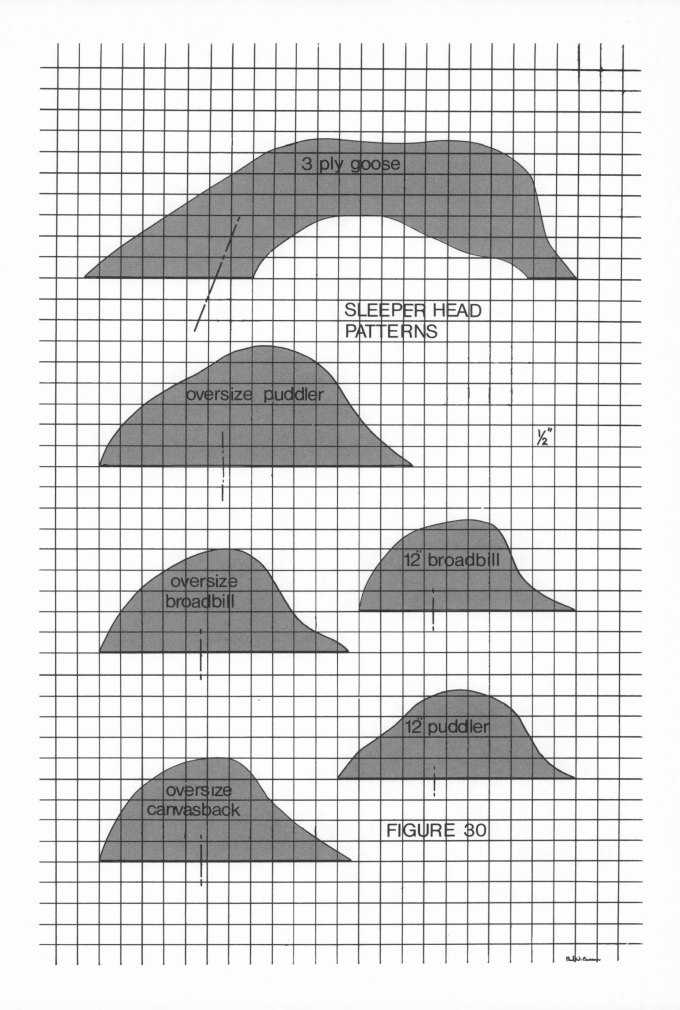

3 ply goose

SLEEPER HEAD
PATTERNS

oversize puddler

½"

oversize
broadbill

12" broadbill

oversize
canvasback

12" puddler

FIGURE 30

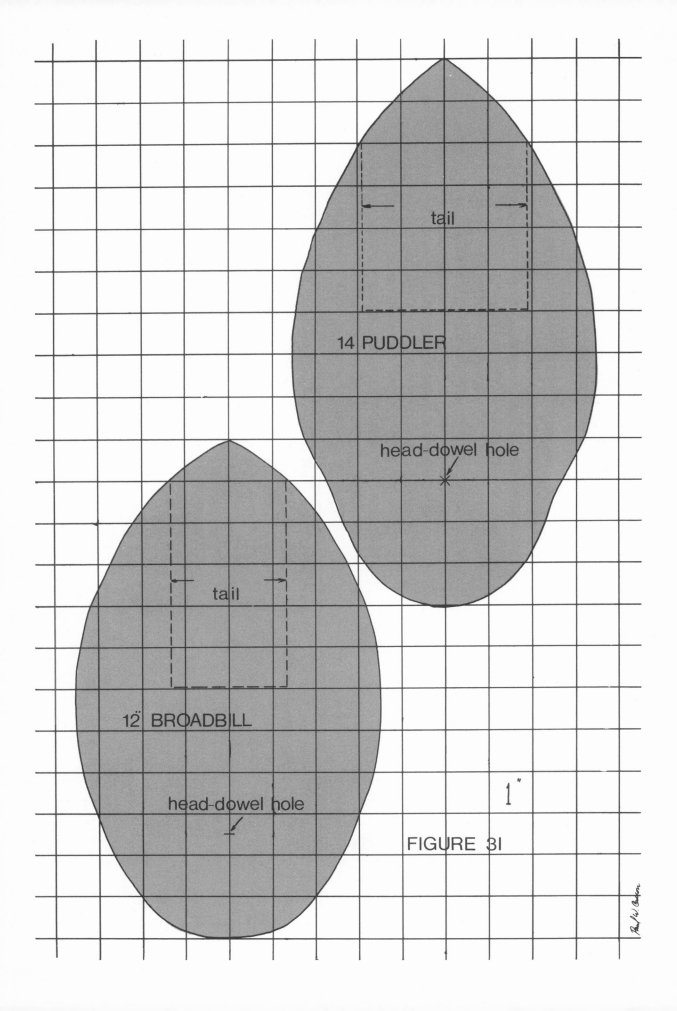

tail

14 PUDDLER

head-dowel hole

tail

12" BROADBILL

head-dowel hole

1"

FIGURE 3I

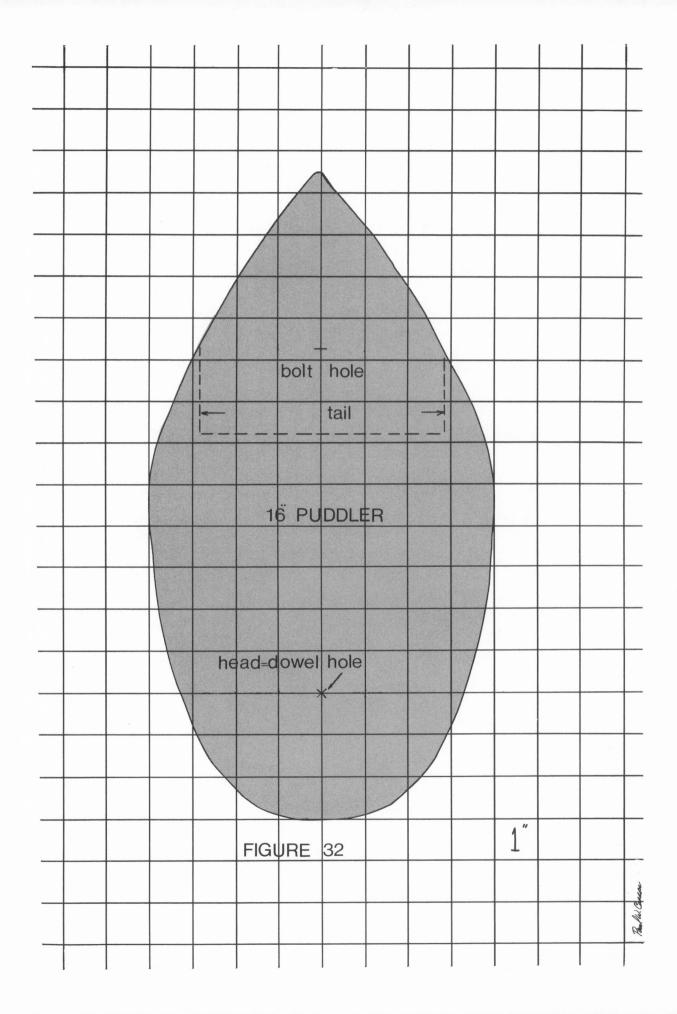

bolt hole

tail

16" PUDDLER

head-dowel hole

FIGURE 32

1"

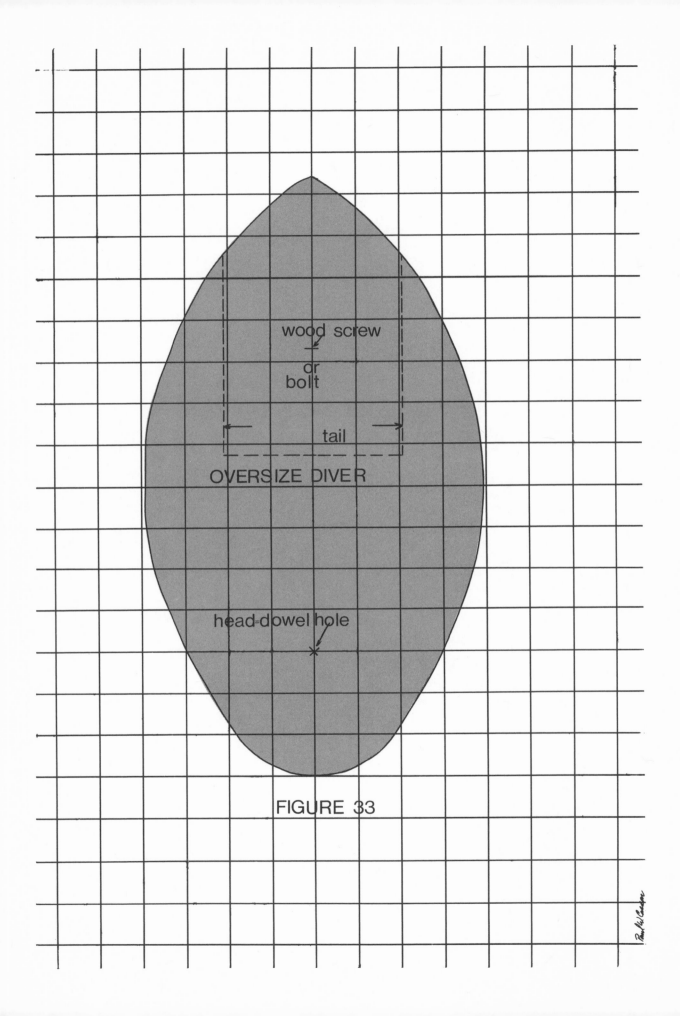

wood screw

or
bolt

tail

OVERSIZE DIVER

head-dowel hole

FIGURE 33

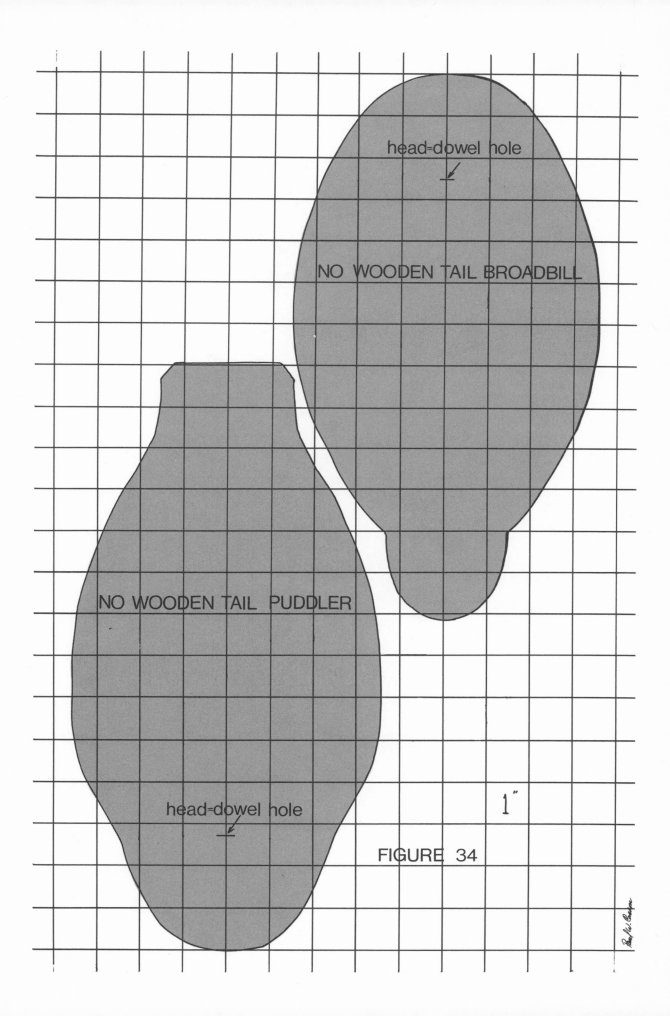

head=dowel hole

NO WOODEN TAIL BROADBILL

NO WOODEN TAIL  PUDDLER

head=dowel hole

1"

FIGURE  34

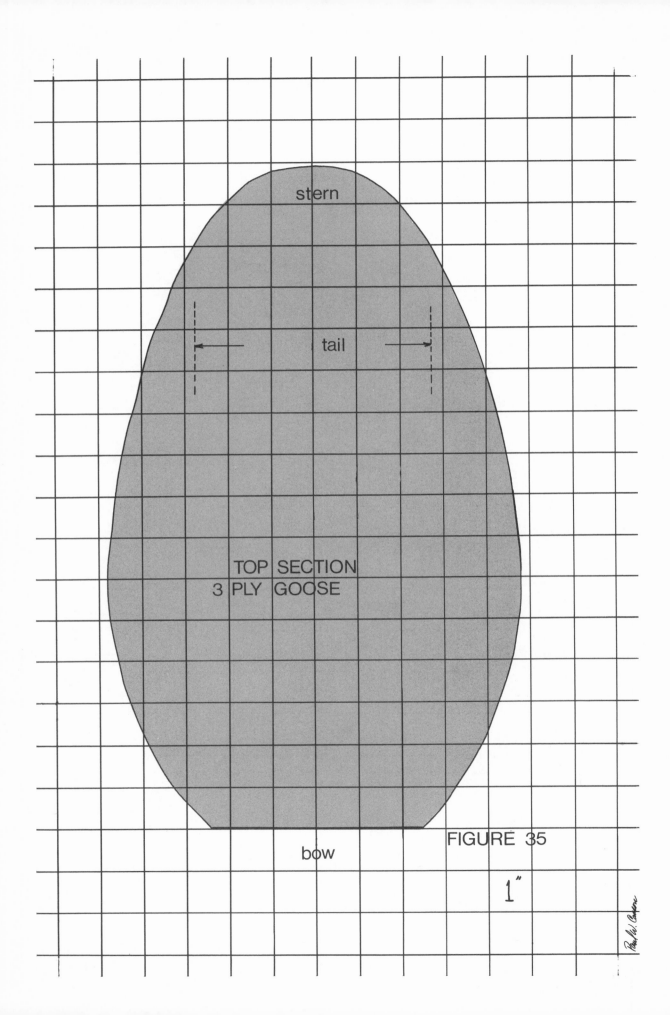

stern

tail

TOP SECTION
3 PLY GOOSE

FIGURE 35

bow

1"

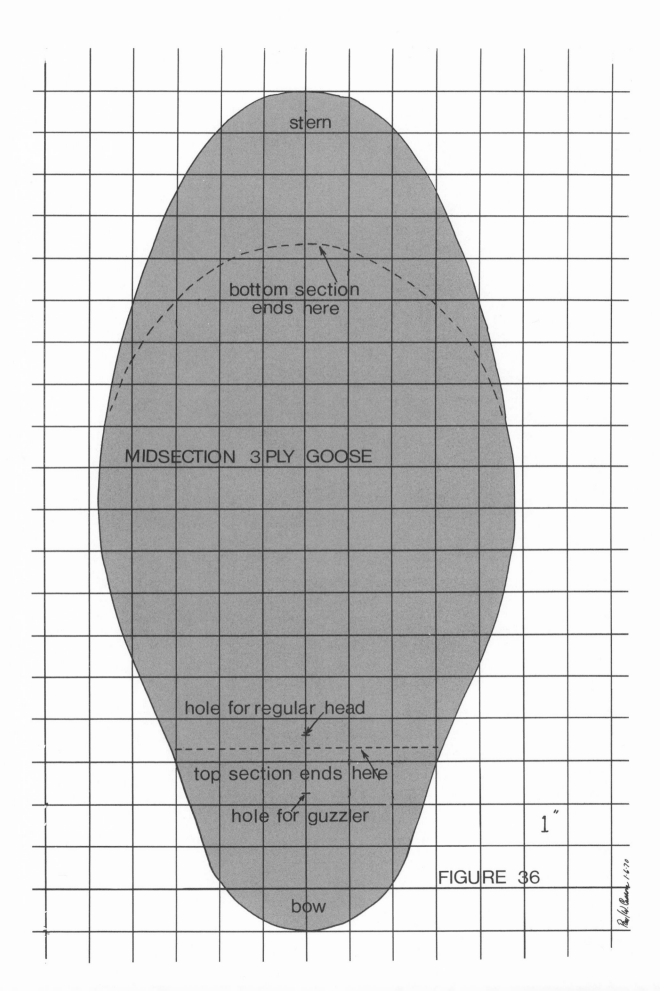

FIGURE 36

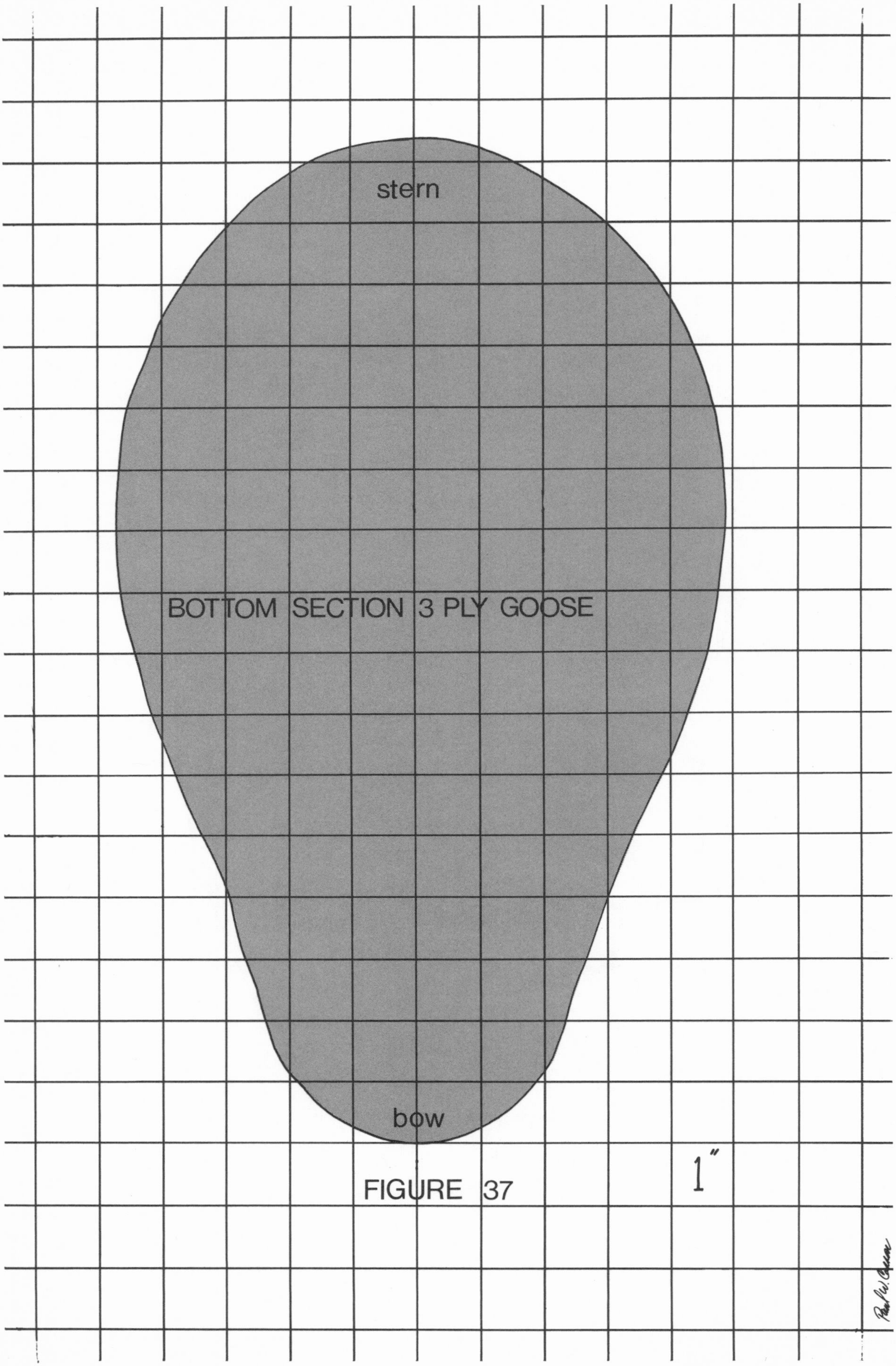

stern

BOTTOM SECTION 3 PLY GOOSE

bow

FIGURE 37

1″

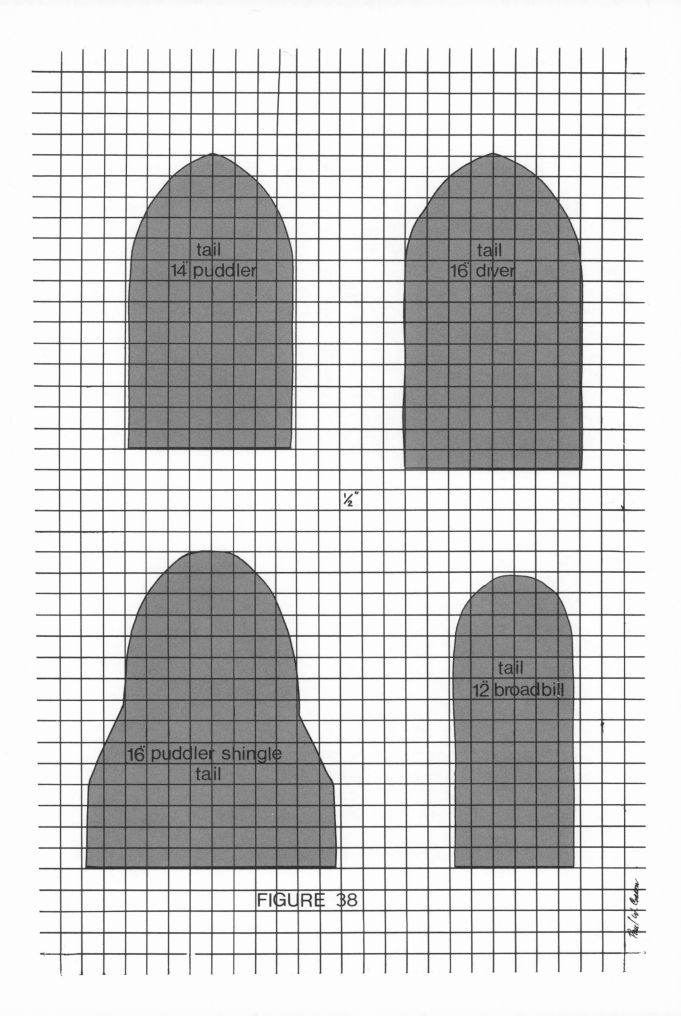

tail
14˝ puddler

tail
16˝ diver

½˝

16˝ puddler shingle
tail

tail
12˝ broadbill

FIGURE 38

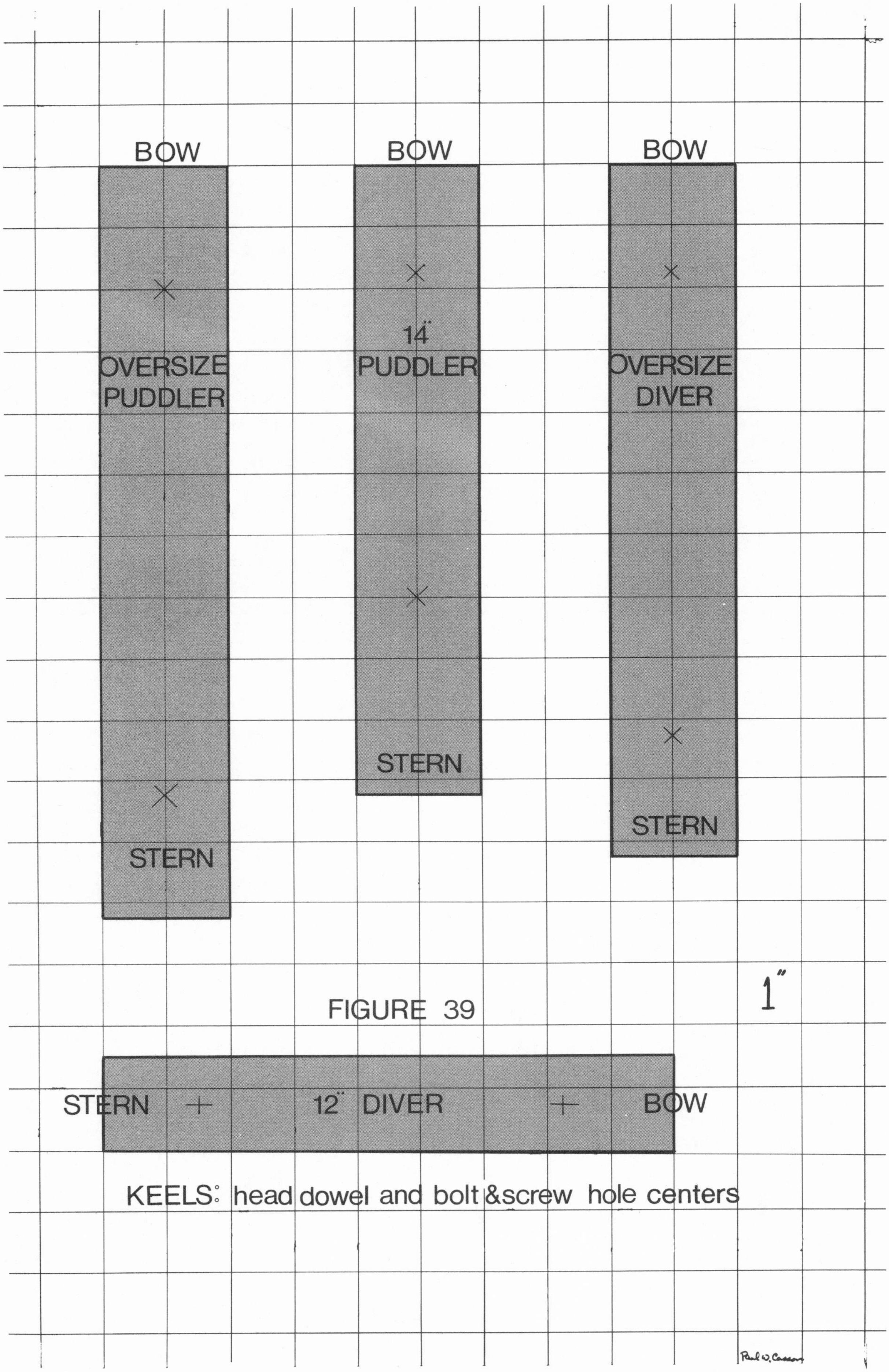

BOW

BOW

BOW

×

×

×

14"

OVERSIZE
PUDDLER

PUDDLER

OVERSIZE
DIVER

×

×

STERN

STERN

×

STERN

FIGURE 39

1"

STERN    +    12" DIVER    +    BOW

KEELS: head dowel and bolt &screw hole centers

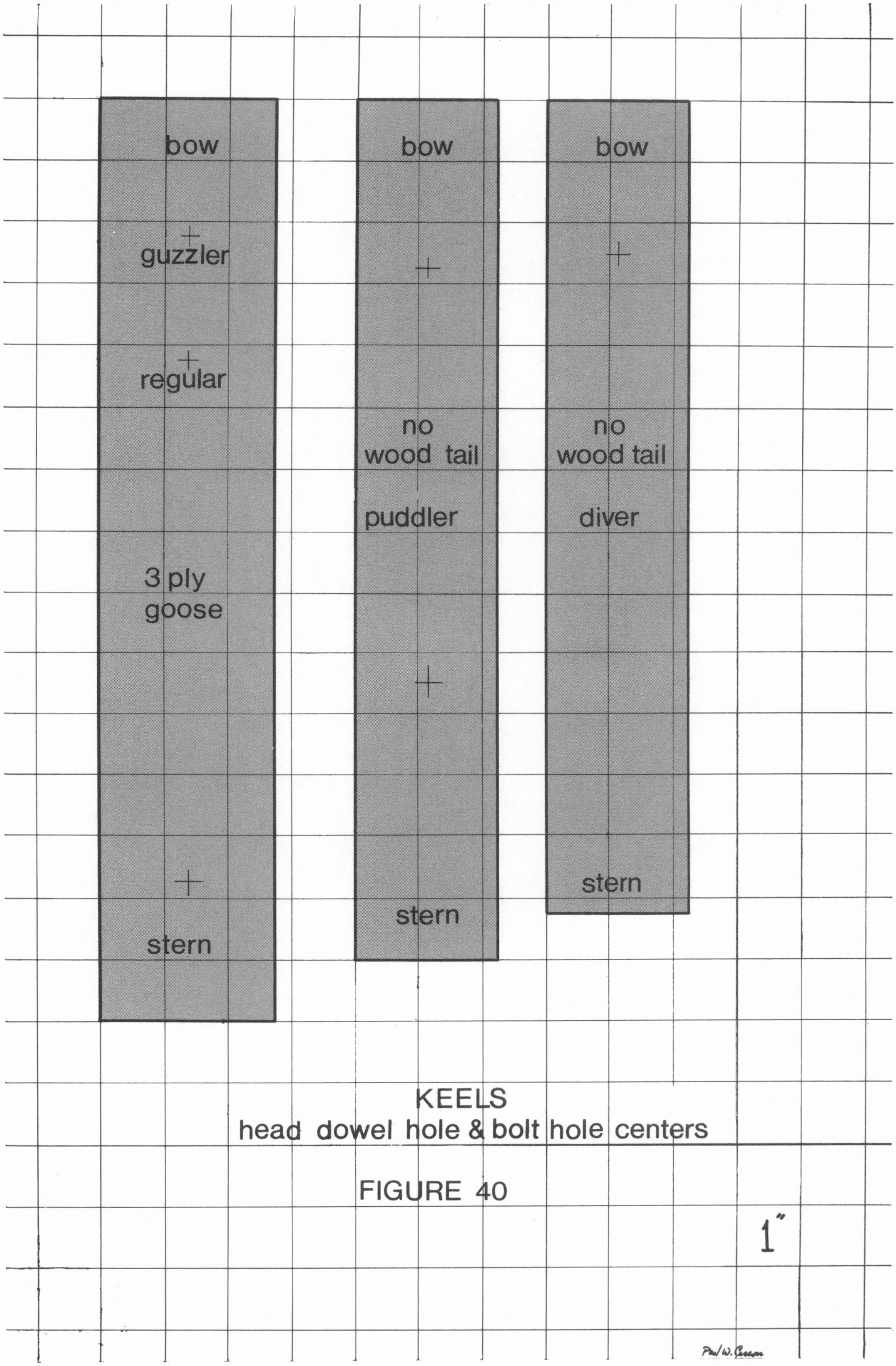
bow
guzzler
regular
3 ply
goose
stern
bow
no
wood tail
puddler
stern
bow
no
wood tail
diver
stern
1"
Paul W. Casson

KEELS
head dowel hole & bolt hole centers

FIGURE 40

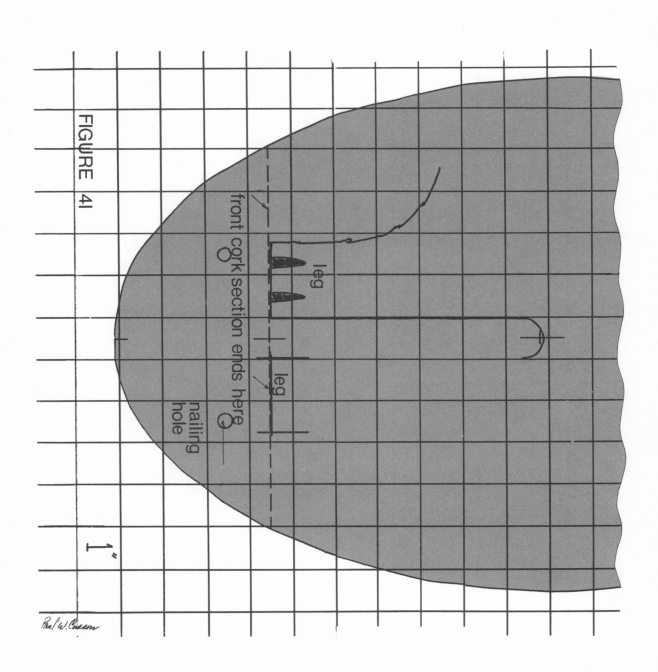

FIGURE 41

front cork section ends here

leg

leg

nailing
hole

1"

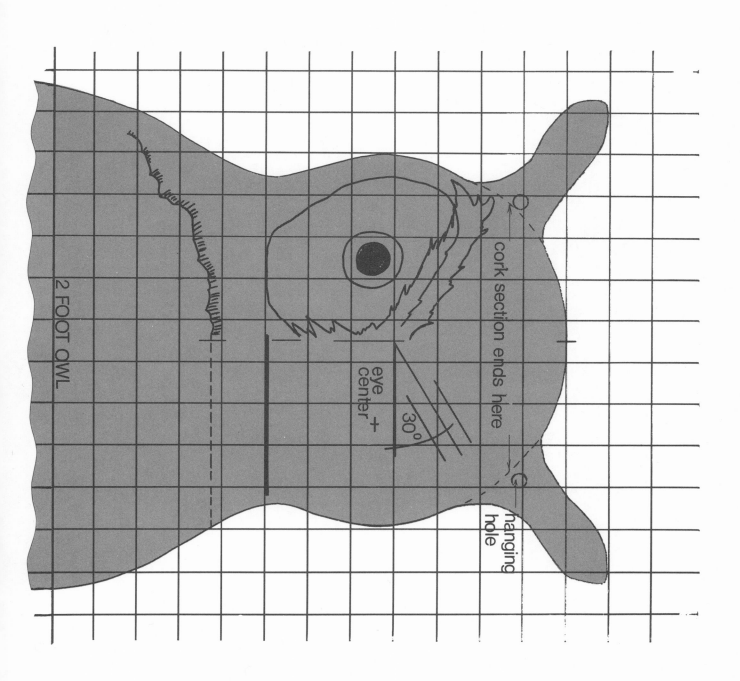

2 FOOT OWL

cork section ends here

eye center +

30°

hanging hole

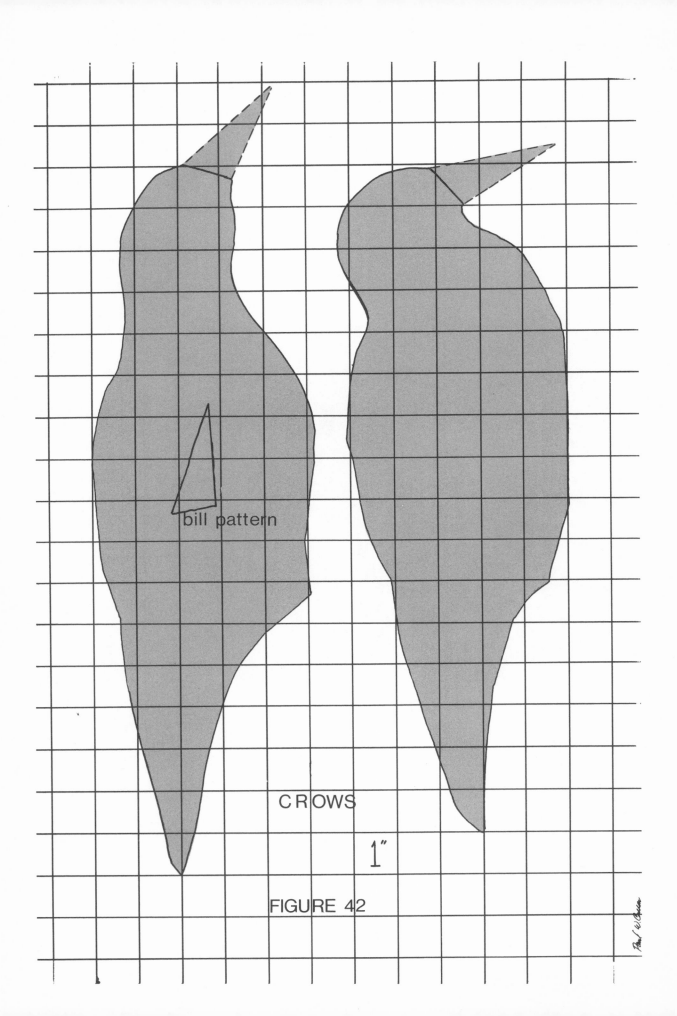

bill pattern

CROWS

1"

FIGURE 42

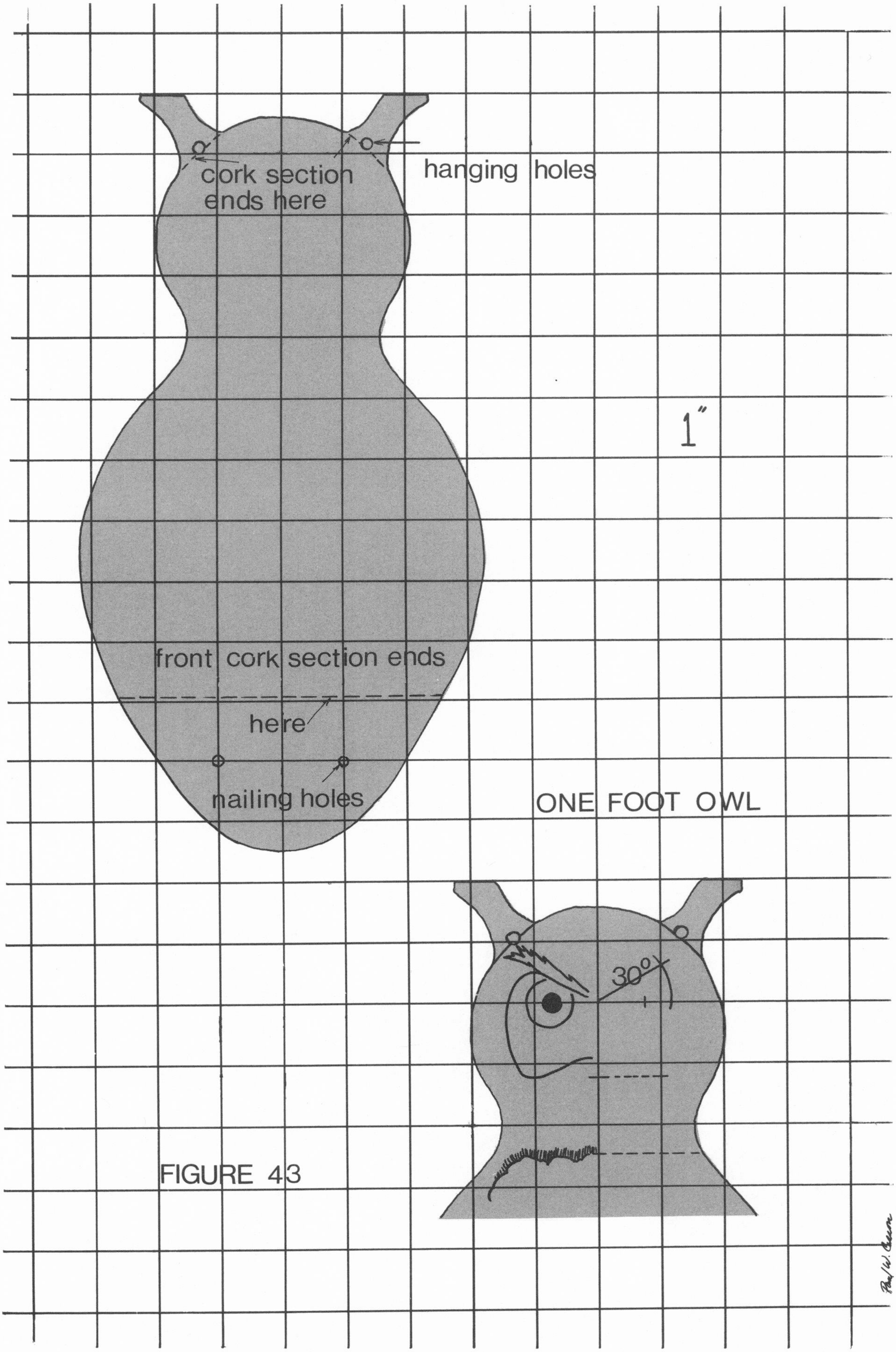

cork section
ends here

hanging holes

1"

front cork section ends

here

mailing holes

ONE FOOT OWL

30°

FIGURE 43